ALISSA MCCLURE

Joy On!

Ten Ways to Add More Joy to Your Life

Westfield Press

This book is dedicated to you. If you are reading this, know that I am grateful. No writer is whole without readers. Thank you for taking this journey with me. I truly hope it brings you more joy.

Contents

Preface

Before we jump into these ten ways to add more joy into our lives, I want to focus on one very important thing: definitions.

Maybe it's the English teacher in me, but I can't discount the value of knowing the definition of a word. Many people use the words "joy" and "happiness" interchangeably, falsely perceiving them as one and the same. For the purposes of this book, here are the words as I will use them:

Joy- a pervasive emotion caused by exceptionally good circumstances; a lasting combination of elation and peace; a blissful state

Happiness- a temporary emotion caused by instant pleasure; momentary contentment; a blissful feeling

Occasional moments of happiness make life fun, but living with joy makes life worthwhile. Our lives were intended to be joyful. This quest for joy is a lifelong quest, because we can always progress and feel greater joy.

You deserve to be joyful! Believe it.

The ten ways that follow can be revisited again and again as you seek to enrich yourself and your life with more and more joy.

Joy on, dear friend.

HOW TO USE THIS BOOK

The intent of this little book was **not** to share ten tips and expect perfection. Such an idea is impossible! This book offers ten ideas for finding more joy in your life. Read through all ten ideas. Not necessarily the additional resources, just start with the initial explanations. It shouldn't take too long. My hope is that **one** of these ten stood out to you the most. This is the **one** you should start with. Go back and read the additional resources included in that chapter. Once you have put your focus on that **one** area of your life for *at least* three weeks, come back to the book and read through the ten again. Chances are, something new will stand out to you. That will be the area you focus on next. Each time you read, my hope is that you will listen to those inner promptings and allow your life to be the life full of joy it was meant to be.

Please do not attempt to do more than one at a time! I know it is tempting. Start with one. If you can't make up your mind, feel free to start with chapter one. You really can't go wrong, as long as you maintain your focus on ONE. *Are you picking up on the theme here?*

Will life be perfect? No. The great thing about joy is that even though we don't have "perfect" lives, we can still have joy. Joy makes difficult times a bit less painful. Always remember, though, that life is full of opposition. Living a joyful life is not a life free of challenges and obstacles. Joy just softens the blows when they come. Because they always come.

*If you find you need a bit more motivation or would prefer a more interactive approach, you can enroll in mini-courses that will walk you through these principles. You can find them at alimcjoy.teachable.com.

1

FORGIVE

Forgive others. Forgive yourself.

During her famous "Lifeclass," Oprah Winfrey quoted a guest on her show who said, "Forgiveness is giving up the hope that the past could be any different." Embrace your current situation and recognize that you are stronger and a better person because of what you learned during those challenging times. As painful as a caterpillar's transformation must be, I am sure that once it emerges from the chrysalis and takes flight, it sees the value in the suffering. When we hold on to our hurt and anger, we are only preventing ourselves from flying.

Challenge: Forgive someone. It can be a large or small offense. It may just be the beginning of the process. But start today and let it go. Releasing those feelings of hurt and anger will feel like you are opening windows and doors to your soul and allowing the light of joy to shine in.

Additional Resources:

The Science of Forgiving

I've always been taught to forgive. But *why?* Forgiving someone else who has hurt us is hard. It is stretching and humbling. For the past month, I have been thinking and studying a lot about forgiving. I have come to understand that forgiving is so much better than holding on to the hurt and pain of anger, no matter how terrible the offense. During her famous "Lifeclass" Oprah Winfrey quoted a guest on her show who said, "Forgiveness is giving up the hope that the past could be any different."

I think sometimes our histories with people (or expectations) make forgiveness all the more challenging. But even though forgiving is challenging (to say the least), it is worth it. Forgiveness is releasing anger and allowing love to replace it. Sometimes when I am stressed I realize that I have been holding my breath. When I stop and exhale and inhale again, I feel refreshed. I think forgiveness works in much the same way. When we stop holding on to the grudge and we invite fresh feelings into our hearts, we feel refreshed.

Dr. Luskin

Dr. Frederic Luskin, the co-founder of the Stanford Forgiveness Project, says, "When you don't forgive you release all the chemicals of the stress response. Each time you react, adrenaline, cortisol, and norepinephrine enter the body. When it's a chronic grudge, you could think about it twenty times a day, and those chemicals limit creativity, they limit problem-solving. Cortisol and norepinephrine cause your brain to enter what we call 'the no-thinking zone,' and over time, they lead you to feel helpless and like a victim. When you forgive, you wipe all of that clean."

Dr. Pietrini

In another study, Dr. Pietro Pietrini at the University of Pisa in Italy found that forgiveness seemed to be a sort of painkiller for moral distress. When he presented his research findings in a 2009 conference, he described them as "evidence that forgiveness likely evolved as a way to overcome pain and alleviate suffering, and that even though it involves parts of the brain responsible for reason, it also requires a counterintuitive, and some would argue, irrational choice: 'You wronged me, but I forgive you, anyway.'"

Dr. Ewin

Dr. Dabney Ewin, a surgeon who specialized in burns, concluded that his patients' anger often interfered with their ability to heal by preventing them from relaxing and focusing on getting better. He began counseling with his patients to help them to forgive, sometimes using hypnosis to help his patients. "What you're feeling will affect the healing of your skin, and we want you to put all your energy into healing," he said.

He would find out what led to their injuries and then he would do hypnosis with them and help them forgive–either themselves or the other person. He would say things like, "You can still pursue damages through an attorney. You're entitled to be angry, but for now I'm asking you to abandon your entitlement and let it go, to direct your energy toward healing, and turn this over to God or nature or whoever you worship. It's not up to you to get revenge on yourself or someone else. When you know at a feeling level that you're letting it go, raise your hand." He said, "Then I'd shut up, they'd raise their hand, and I'd know that a skin graft was gonna take."

{The scientific information shared here is from Megan Feldman Bettencourt's book *Triumph of the Heart: Forgiveness in an Unforgiving World*. An excellent article summarizing ideas from her book can also be found at https://www.salon.com/2015/08/24/the_science_of_forgiveness_when_you_dont_forgive_you_release_all_the_chemi-cals_of_the_stress_response/.}

Love is Not Earned

Isn't it fascinating? As I have been thinking about the concept of forgiveness, however, I had a very powerful thought come to my mind. **We do not love people because they deserve it**. I do not love my children because they have earned my love through some certification process. Instead, I love them because they are my children. For similar reasons, I love my husband and my family members. They do not have to complete a checklist of actions every day in order to earn my love. Forgiveness, I believe, is a form of love.

When we forgive and let go of an offense, we are trading those angry feelings of offense for feelings of love. Obviously I will never love the person who cut me off in traffic or who was rude to be on an airplane more than I love my child, but forgiveness is nonetheless a form of love. As a believer in God, I know that He loves me with a perfect love, even though I am far from deserving of such great and infinite love.

Let It Go, Get It Out

When we choose to let go of hurt and offense, we are choosing to progress. We are choosing to move forward, embracing a future and letting go of past negativity. It is liberating. But we have to choose these actions. They do not happen on their own. If we leave them festering or try to ignore them, they will often repress, but not forever.

When I was at girls' camp one summer, we hiked beside a beautiful stream. Halfway through the hike, we stopped for a lunch break and the leader of the hike told us we could take off our shoes and splash around a little in the shallow water beside the trail. It was a hot, Florida summer day and we all excitedly splashed our feet into the water. While I was walking, I slipped into the clay and a small piece of a stick (just a little thicker than a toothpick and about .25 of an inch long) lodged into the bottom of my heel. It hurt, but I didn't want to make a scene, so I figured when I couldn't get it out on my own right then, I'd mess with it again more when we got back to camp. Surely, I thought, it will come out.

Festering

But walking a few more miles back to camp didn't do me any favors. For the rest of the week I was at camp, I had that little piece of stick lodged into my foot. It hurt, but I could not get it out. In fact, it was hard for me to even really see it because of where it was in my heel. I just kept walking all week, conscious of the annoying little object stuck in my foot, but so distracted by the fun of camp that I didn't do anything to eliminate my problem.

My family was out of town when camp ended, so I went home with a friend and her mom who had been at camp with us. Fortunately her mom was a nurse. When we got back to their home and I wasn't distracted by all the fun activities of camp anymore, I realized that my foot really did hurt. I mentioned it to my mom's friend (after I had cleaned up from camp, of course) and she offered to take a look at it.

She was shocked to see the infected and swollen area on the bottom of my foot and it hurt terribly for her to remove the piece of stick that was now deeply lodged into my heel. The whole time she was working on extracting the stick from my foot (man, it really hurt!), she was reprimanding me for not telling her while we were at camp. She didn't understand why I'd left that little stick in my foot. As I thought about it I realized I didn't know why either. Camp would probably have been even more fun if I hadn't had that annoying pain in my foot the whole time.

Start Healing

So why the gross story about my foot? Because often we do the same thing with offenses. We just leave them there, unresolved, and go about our daily lives. I know I do. We might notice their annoying presence, but we just keep moving along, focusing on other things. When distractions fade, though, and we must face the pain we've been carrying with us, the pain is deeper, and removing it becomes all the more difficult. But difficult is not impossible and healing can and will happen. You may not be able to resolve your problems alone–I know I couldn't get that piece of stick out of my foot without the help of a nurse. There is no shame in seeking help. The deeper the offense, the more time it may take to extract it. The area may have even become infected.

But releasing those feelings allows us to heal–physically and emotionally. We allow joy to replace anger and offense.

How to Forgive: Four Steps to Freedom

Dr. Robert Enright, a developmental psychologist and co-founder of the International Forgiveness Institute, designed forgiveness interventions for therapy. His forgiveness model includes four essential elements:

1-Uncover your Anger

Dr. Frederic Luskin, co-founder of the Stanford Forgiveness Project, says this first step involves teasing apart what he calls "your grievance story." He teaches that when you blame someone else for how you are feeling instead of holding them to account for their actions, you keep yourself stuck in the role of the victim and are trapped by inaction. Luskin encourages participants to "find the impersonal in the hurt" by realizing how many other people have experienced a similar offense or disappointment and how common it is, while acknowledging that most offenses are committed without the intention of hurting anyone personally. Luskin says that even though there is a personal aspect to an offense, acknowledging the possibility of unintentional offense can lessen the pain and blame.

One fantastic way to uncover your anger is through writing. Whether you write in a paper journal or type it into your computer (or any other electronic device), you can dump all of your feelings into words on a page. Let it all out. You do not have to spell correctly or even have logical sentences. Just freewrite whatever comes to your mind. You could even use voice dictation. The point of this exercise is to get the words out of your head and onto a page/screen where you can see them.

When you are finished, you can keep it, rip it into a million pieces, print it and burn it, whatever. But get those words out. Let them work themselves out of your mind and heart and onto something else. The more time you give yourself to write it out, the more you will be able to articulate what you are feeling and why. I often begin such journaling sessions simply as journals but as I realize what is in my heart, I allow my mind to focus there and I try to purge as much of those feelings as I can onto the page. Once they are out of the muddled mess in my head and organized into sentences and paragraphs, I can do more with them. I see them.

2-Decide to Forgive

You must make a conscious decision to forgive someone. It will not "just happen." Yes, you can suppress the memory sometimes, but those pesky offenses always seem to resurface at the most inconvenient times. I don't think that you necessarily have to tell the other person that you are now forgiving them. Often, the other person is oblivious to the offense or may not even be remorseful. You decide. Before you do, however, keep the following questions in mind:

What will telling them accomplish?

Will it make the situation better or worse?

If you are telling your friend that you forgive her for forgetting your birthday after the two of you had made plans the month before, will you only make her feel guilty when she's already got a lot on her mind? Or will this open communication strengthen your friendship and help her understand that birthdays are really important to you?

Whether or not you make your forgiveness public or not, say it out loud or write it down. Take it from an abstract to a concrete action.

"I forgive _____ for _____. "

3-Work on Forgiveness

The offense may be deep and it may have happened so long ago that it has had plenty of time to fester. If so, removal and healing will take time. Start now. You may need to talk to a professional. You will probably need to give yourself time (and an extra dose of patience). Working on forgiveness means consciously progressing daily. Look for the good in your offender(s) and/or your situation rather than focusing on their faults and magnifying their weaknesses. Remember Oprah's quote: "Forgiveness is giving up the hope that the past could be any different." Embrace the present. Be grateful for who you are—the strength and knowledge you've gained–and who you can become.

If you are religious, this is an excellent time to include your efforts in your prayers. Ask for strength. Ask for help. Forgiveness will not happen instantaneously, but it will happen. Our hearts can change, but only if we let them. Incorporating faith into the forgiveness process has enhanced my own efforts exponentially.I often imagine forgiving to be like the proverbial "monkey trap." Sometimes, we have held on to an offense so long, we forget we are even carrying it around with a huge trap. When we slowly uncurl our fingers and let go, we release ourselves from the trap and realize freedom we forgot we were missing. But, sometimes letting go takes time. Muscle memory is real. We must continue working those muscles to get them free. It is not always one quick movement. We might need to stretch and stretch and keep trying until we are finally free.

4-Release from Emotional Prison

When you have finally released your grip and let go of an offense, you can experience greater freedom. This freedom will enable you to do things you did not even imagine were possible. Want to write that novel? Run that marathon? Sing that solo? Paint that painting? The possibilities are endless! When we remove ourselves from the emotional trap and allow ourselves to forgive, we walk away from that pain and invite light and peace and joy into our lives and our souls.

Once the forgiving process has been completed, don't be upset if you don't forget about it. That is normal. We all have scars–physical and emotional ones. Remembering experiences in our lives helps us to prevent similar experiences in the future. For example, I have a burn mark on my leg from carelessly driving and subsequently pulling a riding lawnmower as a teenager. Let's just say I was never careless when I drove the lawnmower again. The same is true with experiences. I remember how it felt to be publicly humiliated by a complete stranger. Because of that pain, even though I have since forgiven said stranger, I will never want to inflict a similar pain on someone else. I am also disinclined to fly to our next family vacation destination.

Don't Give Up

Just like anything else that requires time and effort, we may be tempted to give up. I am here to assure you that the benefits of continued effort far outweigh the costs. Keep trying. Forgiving is worth it. I think it's like giving your soul a flea bath. Maybe you've gotten used to those fleas on your soul, but the minute they are gone, you will notice the peace and be so relieved you are rid of that discomfort.

2

LISTEN

Pause to listen to the people in your life who really matter. Instead of hearing things on the surface, listen for deeper messages. For example, if your daughter has been particularly whiny all week, listen closer to what she is whining about and when she is whining (and don't cop out and say "all the time!"). Maybe she is nervous about change. Maybe she notices that you have been dealing with something stressful lately. Maybe she is growing and her body hurts. Maybe she needs more sleep. Listen.

Listen to your gut instincts.

Listen to music that uplifts. Pay attention to how you feel after watching certain movies. Everyone is different, so quality entertainment for you may not be the same for me. If a particular type of movie leaves you feeling inspired and invigorated, have one ready for those moments when you need an easy pick-me-up.

There is a flip side to this coin. It is important to *not* listen to everything/everyone. Some people are toxic. Some music will really drag you down. Sometimes the overly-critical voices in our own heads need to be ignored until we can get them in check. Just as consciously as you choose to listen to some people and things, be careful that you are not listening to others that will thwart your progress.

Challenge: Choose to listen to your family, friends, and coworkers today. Instead of thinking what you will say next, just listen. Hear what they are saying. Let them know you are listening by looking them in the eyes, nodding, smiling, and affirming them. Feel the joy that comes through truly listening.

Additional Resources:

Sometimes We Don't Need to Listen

Each year for over a decade, I have chosen "One Little Word" to focus on throughout the hear. My One Little Word for 2018 was Listen. I spent the first few months of the year working on listening more to my kids and to friends and family. Maybe one of the best things I've done so far this year is listen to my body and getting a little more sleep. But as I have been considering the importance of listening, some important thoughts have come to my mind that I really want to share. I hope they help bring more joy to your life.

Just as important as choosing to listen to those we love, there are some voices we must choose not to listen to.

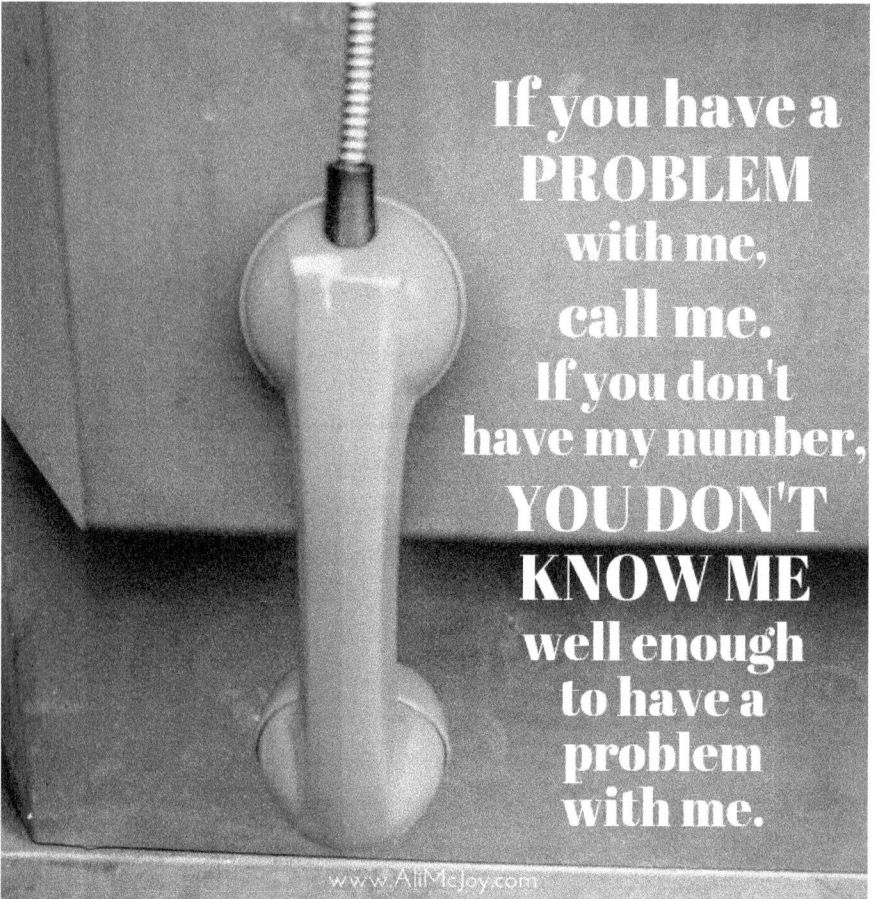

If you have a **PROBLEM** with me, **call me.** If you don't have my number, **YOU DON'T KNOW ME** well enough to have a problem with me.

www.AliMcJoy.com

Don't Listen to Mean People

I was recently listening to one of my favorite podcasts (Awesome with Alison–if you haven't heard it yet, I highly recommend it. I loved her podcasts before, but in December 2017 she was hit by a car and her podcasts full of insights from that experience have now become my favorites.) when I was first inspired to really think about this idea of not listening. In her podcast, Alison shares how a hurtful and negative email really broke her emotionally after her accident. She was devastated by it. It resonated with me because I can think of similar ill-timed negative comments that crumbled me, too. Why do we allow that negativity in?

Sometimes—and for reasons I do not understand—people just feel the need to be mean. Usually it is because they are hurting, too, so they lash out in pain. Most members of the human race do this at least once in their lives. Acknowledging that helps us to take some of the venom from the sting, but the sting remains. We have to stop listening to people who are lashing out. We cannot be their victims. We are victors!

Hear, But Don't Listen

It's like being surrounded by smoke you don't inhale.

Or, strive to listen to the message a person is trying to convey beyond the actual words he is using. For example, I have a son who gets HANGRY. You know what I'm talking about, right? His blood sugar dips a little bit and look out world! No one is safe. I have come to recognize that when he begins his angry rants, he doesn't mean the actual words that are coming out of his mouth (they are usually pretty cruel). What he is actually conveying to me is that he is hungry. We are working on helping him to recognize those feelings before things get too bad. I think we are making progress. Hopefully we will master this before he gets much older. But my point is I have chosen to not get offended and take his lashing out personally.

Don't Listen to the Negative Voice Inside Your Head

Do you have this problem? I do! A few years ago, I heard someone ask, "Why do we allow ourselves to say horrible things to ourselves that we would never allow our children to say to anyone?" That struck a chord with me because I have worked hard to teach my children not to say words like stupid or fat. In fact, sometimes my kids come home and say something like, "Mom, a boy said the "s word" today at school," and I know they mean "stupid" and not the real "s word." It makes me smile

(I know the clock is ticking on that innocence, so I am in no hurry to correct it!).

For most of my life I had been saying phrases like, "I'm so stupid!" or in recent years (since having kids), "I'm so fat!" These phrases weren't doing anybody any favors. So I took the challenge from said wise person to stop saying–and even thinking–these negative phrases. Instead I say comments like, "Oops!" or "That was a silly mistake!" or "Silly Mommy!" More than once I have heard one of my kids say, "Silly Mommy" or "Silly me!" when they see me or themselves make a mistake. My hope is that these words will help reduce the negativity in their own heads, too. I know it's made a big difference for myself.

Give Yourself a Boost

Fresh out of college, I attended a fantastic leadership meeting. During the meeting, one of the speakers began by saying, "Good evening! How are you?" And then he waited for responses. Some people said "OK," someone shouted, "TIRED!" and then lots of various answers started coming. Once the answers died down, he asked us, "Do you think that the person who asks you how you are doing is really stopping to listen the majority of the time?"

We stopped to think about it. He then said, "I believe that when someone asks you how you are doing, they are actually giving you an opportunity to give yourself a boost." He explained that when we answer that question negatively, we are telling ourselves that things are bad. We send ourselves into a negative spiral. But if we take that opportunity to say that things are great or that we are having the best day of our lives, we are giving ourselves a mental boost. We are thrusting ourselves forward, giving a positive spin to our day, and subsequently, to our lives. For almost 15 years now I have applied this thinking to my life and I can attest that it is absolutely true.

Keeping it Real

Now, if I am having the worst day ever and a dear friend sits down and is genuinely talking to me, I am not going to lie and say that I am great. But if I am walking down the sidewalk and I see an acquaintance who says, "How's it going?" I'll say, "Great!" and keep walking. I am always glad I did. Try it! It really does give you a more positive outlook. It is a great way to change the dynamic of an ordinary day.

So...how are you doing today?

Impostor Syndrome

I try to attend my local chapter meetings for the Society of Children's Book Writers and Illustrators. During one such meeting, the presenter shared quite a few things about the science of brain research and how those things influence us as writers. There were a lot of very interesting points brought up about neuro-pathways and the evidence that intelligence is malleable. Do you want to know what seemed to resonate most with everyone in the room?

Impostor's Syndrome

Impostor's Syndrome. Everyone felt compelled to share their experiences with this and how they are always fighting to overcome it (or some shared how they want to be fighting it).

This got me thinking. In a room full of people who are living their dreams and publishing books, why would so many feel like imposters? Why would they feel like they are not deserving of the praise they receive? Why do we so often brush off compliments and believe that people are just "being nice"?

The entire evening and into this morning, I couldn't help but think about how prevalent Impostor's Syndrome is. My mind kept coming back to two inspiring responses to Impostor's Sydrome.

Inspiring Words to Combat Impostor's Syndrome

The first comes in the form of some inspiring words from Marianne Williamson. When I was teaching middle school, I used to print copies of this and share it with my students as our "Quote of the Day" for our last day of school.

> *"Our deepest fear is not that we are inadequate. Our deepest fear is that we are powerful beyond measure. It is our light, not our darkness that most frightens us. We ask ourselves, 'Who am I to be brilliant, gorgeous, talented, fabulous?' Actually, who are you not to be? You are a child of God. Your playing small does not serve the world. There is nothing enlightened about shrinking so that other people won't feel insecure around you. We are all meant to shine, as children do. We were born to make manifest the glory of God that is within us. It's not just in some of us; it's in everyone. And as we let our own light shine, we unconsciously give other people permission to do the same. As we are liberated from our own fear, our presence automatically liberates others."*

Who Am I?

Isn't this quote a breath of fresh air? I often ask myself that question, "Who am I to be successful? Who am I to _____?"

I enjoy singing. Occasionally I sing solos at events and every time, my fear comes immediately after I start to sing. I think, "Who am I to do this well?" All the air in my body disappears with those first two or three notes and the subsequent notes leave me gasping for breath. I don't feel like I recover till I am about halfway through the song–if ever.

The response in the quote is so great. "Who are you not to be?" I am a firm believer that we were all created by the same Creator. We are all equally loved by Him. So why is it that I think it is OK for other people to share their talents and do amazing things, yet I shrink when it is my turn? This quotation, for me, is the cure. If I really want to help anyone, if I really want to make the world a better place (and don't we all?), I must let my own light shine. When I do, I am giving you, and everyone within our vicinity, permission to do the same. Let your light shine! That light is the empowering force that will liberate us all from this crippling Impostor's Syndrome.

Inspiring Example to Combat Impostor's Syndrome

The second example comes from one of the most humble men I've ever known. He came from a very poor upbringing and lived a full life. He left school in 8th grade. But he worked hard every day of his life. He never shied away from trying new–and seemingly impossible–things because he didn't feel "qualified." Instead he just did what he thought needed to be done.

I watched this man establish a barbeque restaurant with a friend. He was always repairing things and building things he wasn't "qualified" to repair or build, out of necessity. I saw him work his way into a chef's kitchen at a world-renowned restaurant. I witnessed him figure out how best to cover enormous trees in Christmas lights with a bucket truck. He did such an impressive job, even our local towns asked him to help decorate their trees. I worked with him (as did my younger siblings) as we followed his instructions and built a garage onto the side of our house, complete with stucco and all. We had no Internet resources or YouTube videos. He led us as if he knew what he was doing and he did the jobs that had to be done, without pausing for self-doubt.

Failure is Inevitable

Not all of his projects were successes. He once decided he wanted to convert a shower into a big bathtub, so he created it with concrete. It worked, but it was definitely not pretty or comfortable. But he was happy with the results. W.H. Auden said, "The chances are that, in the course of his lifetime, the major poet will write more bad poems than the minor, simply because major poets write a lot." The more we get out and try, the more outcomes we will have. Yes, we will have more failures than if we didn't try at all, but we will also have more successes.

I think of this man, my stepdad, and his example to me often. He was not perfect. None of us is. But he didn't let his limitations stop him from doing amazing things in his lifetime. He didn't pretend to be an expert or go around bragging about his accomplishments to everyone he met. He just kept trying new things as different needs arose. His example has blessed me in my own life.

So as I sit here at my desk, my eyes a little cloudy with emotion as I think about his profound influence in my life, I am full of gratitude. I am grateful for him. Even though he passed away over five years ago, his legacy lives on. I can't count the number of times he would call me over to the piano and ask me to sing for guests in our home. His opinion was, if you can do something, do it and don't be ashamed. And so I, though unqualified as I feel, will continue to sing. I will continue to write, not because I feel "qualified," but because it is where my heart is. It is a part of who I am. I hope I will someday liberate others as I let my light shine.

Consider these two questions:
How do you deal with Impostor's Syndrome?
What can you do to let your light shine?

3

BUDGET

O ne of the areas that can quickly steal our joy is FINANCES. The vast majority of the world stresses about money matters. One of the best ways to eliminate that stress is by budgeting. If you cringed just now, hear me out: If you were stranded on a deserted island for a week with a limited amount of food, you would plan that food carefully–right?–so you would have enough to get by until you knew you were not going to starve. Money is the same way. Make a plan with what you have so you are sure your priorities are covered until you get more money. Be consistent and conscientious. Spending isn't inherently bad, if you do it intentionally. Former Vice President Joe Biden said, "Don't tell me what you value. Show me your budget and I'll tell you what you value." If you haven't aligned your spending with your priorities yet, there's no time like the present. It will bring more peace and joy to your life than guessing.

Challenge: Start today by considering your financial bucket list. What do you want your money to do for you? Take those ideas as your motivation to continue moving forward and get control over your life. If you are married, include your spouse in your daydreams as you create your financial bucket lists.

Additional Resources:

What a Suitcase Has to Do With Budgeting

In recent years I have been put a lot more effort into being more organized and educated about our family's finances than ever before. I read close to 20 book (seriously) on the subject over the course of one year and read countless other articles and listened to hours and hours of podcasts.

I have taught a few Family Finance classes to groups of adults in our area. I absolutely love seeing people empowered by the control they gain over their money! It's a beautiful thing.

As I was preparing to teach my second group about budgeting, I had this epiphany and I like it so much I thought I'd share it here, too!

So often we think of budgeting as this miserable drudgery that just reminds us of how far we are from where we want to be—I know I did. Let's change that mindset:

Budgeting is like packing a suitcase for travel.

Before you pack your suitcase, you need to know a few things. You can't just start gathering up stuff in a pile and expect to pack the right stuff. So we have a few questions we need to ask ourselves:

   –Where am I going? What do I want to do when I get there?

   –When am I going and for how long?

   –How I am traveling? Bus? Airplane? Car?

   –How big is my suitcase?

Once we know where we are planning to go and what it is we want to do, we can envision some of the things we will need. Maybe we are planning to return with some souvenirs, so we'll need to take that into consideration when we are packing and leave space for them. When I teach the Family Finances course, our first day of class ends with each class member completing a Financial Bucket List sheet (inspired by Lauren Greutman's book *The Recovering Spender*). I love this activity because each person gets to dream. Then we go home and each couple talks about their financial bucket lists together and they compare notes and share dreams and discuss what they want to do with their combined future. It can be a really strengthening exercise for a couple, but also a motivating experience for an individual. The bucket list helps you to consider your long-term goals and dreams and help you see where you want to go. Seeing the big picture helps put day-to-day decisions in perspective. It answers the questions Where am I going? and What do I want to do when I get there?

Am I going next week? Next month? Next year? How long will I be gone? My suitcase will be different if I am packing summer clothes or winter clothes, right? If I'm going to be gone for one week or four, I may choose different outfits and different quantities of items. As we consider timing and current needs, we can prepare for them. I am a big-time list maker. When I am planning to travel, I make a list of all of the things I know I need to pack and as ideas come, I add them to my list. This helps me stay organized and keeps me from forgetting important things as I pack my bags intentionally.

Each method of travel imposes different restrictions and requirements. We all have restrictions imposed on us, right? Are we paying off lots of debt? Are we paying lots of medical bills? Are there certain things we just can't buy right now? Sure! That's the nature of traveling down any path:if you are trying to hike a trail down the Grand Canyon, you stay on the trail. You can't simultaneously go down into the Grand Canyon and climb Mount Everest. Choose your destination, find the path that will get you there, and then STICK TO IT!

How big is my suitcase? It is so crucial to know how much income you have coming in each month. You can't move forward without knowing this. Sometimes we think we know, or we have an "idea," but that is not enough. You need to know to the penny how much money you are brining in each month. Is your suitcase expandable? Know your pre-tax income and see if you are overpaying in taxes each year. If you receive a big tax refund each year, chances are you are overpaying in taxes each pay check. Talk with someone in your HR department about making that correction and it will be as if you just unzipped the expansion on your expandable suitcase. Once you know how big your suitcase is, you can begin packing.

When we pack, we start with the essentials. I want to make sure I have clothes, underwear, deodorant, toothbrush and toothpaste, contacts and contact solution, a hairbrush, socks, shoes, and a phone charger. If my suitcase is small, I may be bringing only a trial size of contact solution or a fewer amount of clothes that I will have to wash while I am traveling. I can't just keep piling stuff into or on top of my suitcase and expect it all to arrive safely at my destination. In fact, many times overstuffed suitcases come open or break apart during travel (Have you ever seen a broken suitcase coming around the conveyor belt in a big, clear, plastic bag? I cringe every time hoping it's not mine!). We can only pack what will fit, so we start with what we need the most. This concept is also true when we are budgeting. We can't spend money we don't have (It's really not an option—remember what happened to the suitcase? It ain't pretty.), so we start with the things that are most important first: food, rent/mortgage, electricity, and water. Then we add more if there is still space. Have you ever noticed that it doesn't seem to matter how big your suitcase is you always seem to fill it? I think that is often true with our finances as well: regardless of whether we make a lot of money or a little, we use it all. It all depends on how and what you pack. If you are careful with the space in your suitcase, you will have enough space to bring all the things you need and a few extra things you want as well. Nobody's carrying a suitcase big enough to hold a kitchen sink, so don't consume yourself with the idea that you need a suitcase that big. Instead, focus on the space you do have and then utilize that space as best you can. Maybe down the road you will get a bigger suitcase, but in the meantime, you haven't broken the one that you have from overfilling it.

This mindset is so empowering. As you move forward each paycheck packing intentionally, you will get to every destination you desire.

Confessions of a Natural-Born Spender

I'll admit it: I am a spender. I cringe at the thought of money lazing in a savings account day after day. Bank crashes may actually be an existing, albeit illogical, fear of mine. At the same time, though, I don't consider myself an impulse-buyer, either. I research my decisions and I read reviews, ask around, and subscribe to Consumer Reports. I watch for sales and coupons and pay attention to the season when I make important purchases. With almost every purchase, I shop around and base my decisions on a combination of factors including quality, price, customer service, and company ethics. But, alas, I am still a spender, and I have felt guilty about my spending nature for most of my life. Can a spender be a spender and still succeed financially? Yes!

My Aunt Norene was amazing at saving money. She and her husband had saved tons of money during their working lifetime and were able to retire in their fifties and move to Florida, never to worry about finding a job again. She was a real penny-pincher, though, and when I was a girl, her thriftiness seemed almost unbearable to me. Now that I am an adult, I can't help but admire her incredible self-discipline.

As I have journeyed over the course of the past year and a half, learning as much as I can about personal (and family) finance, I have come to learn two life-changing concepts that are good for this spender's soul. They have really helped me shift my mindset without completely rewiring my brain. If you, too, are a natural-born spender, or know someone who is, I hope these two concepts help you like they've helped me.

1-Spending money isn't inherently bad.

We have grown up thinking that spending money is the antithesis of saving. Nope. Failure to have a plan (as in budget) is the real antithesis of saving. If you are flying by the seat of your pants and spending money (even sparingly) without a plan, you are slowing down your ability to save. Why? Because expenses will always arise. If you do not already have a plan in place and money allocated to cover those expenses, as well as money you intentionally allocate towards future expenses (as in savings), you will thwart your savings goals. If I want to spend money, that is OK, as long as I stay within the bounds I have set for myself. When I intentionally set aside $1000 for a small 3-day trip to San Diego, I am doing that on purpose and I can continue to responsibly allocate money to my other expenses, including future expenses. When I am intentional with my money, I don't have to feel guilty for making purchases I have planned on that align with my priorities.

2-Saving is actually future spending.

You may have picked up on it already, but I had to state it anyway. Instead of thinking of my money as fresh fruits rotting away in an unknown place, I can recognize that I am allocating my money into categories that I may not need today, but I will need in the future and when that future date comes, I will be so glad to have that money! When I give my money specific jobs, even if those jobs will be completed in the future, I feel satisfied that my money has been "spent" and is not merely sitting there "rotting." I know this sounds illogical to you savers out there who relish the idea of saving money and stockpiling it for those rainy days, but I am who I am. Sorry if it doesn't make sense to you!

You Can Control Your Money, Not Everything

Could the bank still potentially crash and keep all my money? Maybe, but I try not to focus on that (FDIC anybody?)! Instead, I revel in the peace of mind that comes daily from being in control of my money. I can tell my money what to do instead of feeling tossed to and fro by the winds and storms of everyday life. Bank hacks happen. Cars break down. Furniture needs to be replaced. Foods get eaten. But if we plan for those expenses, we will be OK. Actually, OK is an understatement. Sometimes people make comments like, "I don't have time or energy to budget." Friends, let me assure you that the time and energy you are wasting on trying to fumble through life without a financial plan is infinitely more than the amount of time and energy it takes to maintain a budget.

If you haven't tried maintaining a budget (which includes some forecasting, allocating, and accounting), try it! If you don't enjoy the peace of mind that comes with it, you can always quit and go back.

What about paying down debt? How does that work for a spender?

Undisciplined spenders accrue debt. It is easy to do, trust me. I know. But once I recognized what a huge chunk of our income was going toward old spending, limiting the amount of spending we could do with our current money, it didn't take me long to want to rush our way out of debt. Think about it: if you are paying a car payment and multiple credit card payments and student loan payments and store credit payments, a HUGE chunk of your spending power is tied up in spending you did in the past. This makes it nearly impossible to spend your money on the things that really matter to you, now and in the future. Even if your interest rate is super low, the payment still exists. Knock it out! Make a plan and power through your debt as fast as you can. Basically, you feel like you are buying freedom. You will love the freedom you feel and the options—oh the options!

A Spender on a Budget

There you have it. I am a spender. I will probably always be a spender. But if I can give myself spending limits (Lauren Greutman compares them to a backyard fence that gives limits to keep you and your family securely within the boundaries of your own yard), and plan for future spending, I will have the money I need when I need it–and isn't that the whole point?

4

ESCAPE

You can't run away from your problems, but you *can* find a mental escape in doing something you love.

Find an activity that you enjoy doing that enriches your life. Whether you choose knitting, drawing, painting, running, reading, writing, sewing, dancing, singing, playing an instrument, learning something new, volunteering, playing a sport, hiking, kayaking, or anything else that appeals to you, the idea is CHOOSE SOMETHING!

Now once you have chosen something, choose a time that you will dedicate to doing that thing. When that time comes, do it. Continue scheduling time that is specifically for the thing(s) you enjoy. Obviously, you can't schedule hours every day to only do the things you want to do. There are so many other commitments nagging at your time. The important thing to remember is that we all need to escape reality sometimes. So, stop being a martyr and plan regular times for you to do your chosen activity before reality gets to be too much.

When I am doing something that I enjoy and scheduling it as a mandatory part of my day, I realize I don't feel quite so trapped in the shackles of adulthood anymore. Doing this doesn't make me become a selfish woman who spends her whole day only thinking about myself, but instead helps me to gain focus and mental clarity. By spending that time (for me, it's typically early early in the morning before my family wakes up) doing something that brings me joy, I can share that joy all day long with my family and friends and those with whom I interact along the way.

Challenge: Spend a few minutes (these could be minutes while driving or cleaning if you don't feel like you have time to just sit still for a few minutes to think) thinking about what it was you enjoyed doing when you were younger. Are any of those things missing in your life now? Do you miss any of them? If so, identify how you could incorporate that into your life. Commit to doing something related to that thing you enjoy for the rest of the week. Consider how you could do something related to your activity daily.

Additional Resources:

Finding An Escape Without Abandoning Your Family

I read an article in REAL SIMPLE magazine entitled *The Escape Plan*. In it, author Janelle Brown talks about how common it is for people–women in particular–to fantasize about running away or escaping their current lives and living out some carefree dream. Michelle Obama shares in her book *Becoming* that her mother daydreamed about leaving every spring after surviving another Chicago winter. I admit that I, too, have had daydreams of leaving behind all of the stress and responsibility of my everyday life. Brown hits the nail on the head when she says, "...life seems to come with an ever-growing set of restrictions. The trappings of adulthood that you aspire to—a career, a home, a partner, kids, pets—also happen to cut back on your freedom."

One of my twins week seems to constantly be talking about how he can't wait to be a grown-up. It's the age-old cycle, isn't it? Children wish for adulthood and adults pine for childhood. I tried to explain to him how much he should appreciate the fun and carefree life he gets to lead as a child and how much obligation and work there is in being an adult, but he shrugged it all off and said, "At least you get to do whatever you want." I laughed out loud! I just looked at him and said, "Son, take a guess at how often I get to do whatever I want. If I could do whatever I wanted right now, I'd be taking a nap!" But even as these words came out of my mouth, I heard a sort of internal reprimand saying, "Whose fault is that?" I am not a martyr. Sometimes I say this as a mantra:

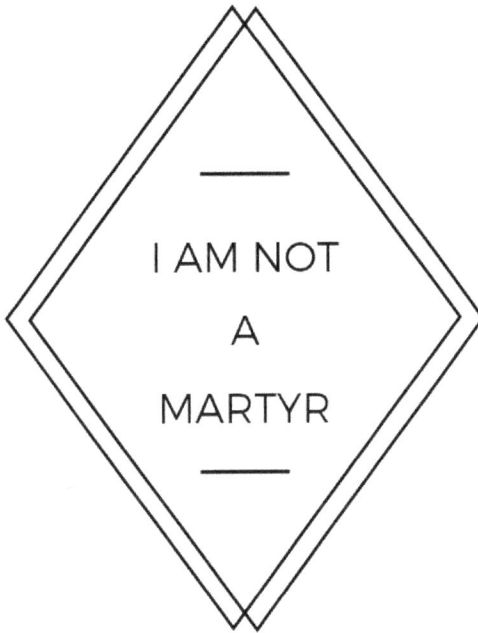

I AM NOT

A

MARTYR

This is one major reason why I write: because I want to. Because it is something I want to do instead of the myriad of things I have to do. So what if I'm not the best at it or if I never receive millions of dollars or prestigious awards for my writing? That's not why I am doing it. I am writing because I want to. And when I am doing something that I enjoy and scheduling it as a mandatory part of my day, I realize I don't feel quite so trapped in the shackles of adulthood anymore.

So instead of threatening to drive to the grocery store and never return (I have totally whispered to my husband, "I may not come back" before), I can escape into a good book, learn something new, or write it out in a journal entry or a blog post or my next book. These all work for me.

Knowing that is empowering and helps push me to do things that I enjoy on a regular basis, simply because I enjoy them. Doing this doesn't make me become a selfish woman who spends her whole day only thinking about herself, but instead helps me to gain focus and mental clarity. By spending that time (for me, it's typically early early in the morning before my family wakes up) doing something that brings me joy, I can share that joy all day long with my family and friends and those I interact with along the way.

I reached out to my friend Jo who runs a website called LetsKeep-Running.com and she said, "I feel so much better and am therefore a better mom when I exercise every day—but I need to run every week too! There's just something about being outside and my feet pounding the pavement—it's very cathartic for me, and helps me feel grounded. It's also someplace I can push myself and accomplish goals outside of parenting."

So today, my friend, I ask you: what do you do to escape? If you haven't thought about it before (or for a LONG time), please take a few minutes (**right now, go ahead, I'll wait**) to think about it now. I know runners who feel as if they are escaping when they go for a run, is that you? I know artists who escape into their drawings/paintings/sculptures/poetry/music, is that you? I know people who love to be outdoors, is that you?

There are so many great things you could choose from, just remember that what works for you will not necessarily be the same as anyone else. Don't choose something because it is trendy or because you think it sounds important. Don't choose an escape because you think it will be lucrative. Choose something that resonates with **you** and then schedule time to do it sometime this week. I would love to hear what you choose and how you feel! Post a picture on Instagram and use *#joyon!* or share it on my Facebook page so we can all see!

For me, when I step out of my little office, I close the door behind me and echo the sentiments of Janelle Brown: "I may be shackled to this life, with all of its dizzying highs and lows, and yet I could not possibly live without my captors."

5

SERVE

S erving others is *the* way to find true and lasting happiness. But serving others does not have to be a huge, official ordeal with lots of preparation and logged hours. Serving others can be as big or as small as you have time and energy for. If you only have a few minutes, or no time at all, consider committing to smile at every person you see (more than once, I have been thanked by strangers in public places for smiling at them). If you are planning to be home with your little ones (and they are healthy), consider inviting someone else over to join you. If you have a relative in a distant city to whom you haven't talked in a while, call her!

You can read to kids, donate books, donate clothes, help a neighbor with a difficult chore, pick up trash, volunteer at a zoo/ library/ school/ hospital, or make a meal for someone.

When we invite that spirit of service into our lives, we instantly feel more joy. Don't let the service stress you out. If your day is insanely busy, plan a small act of service like a kind text message to a friend/relative. Allow your heart and mind to be open to service. You will find opportunities that will fit into your routines and schedule.

The last time I flew alone, I vowed to be on the lookout for any mothers traveling alone with kids. I went out of my way to help (without seeming like a creeper, of course...it's a fine line). One mom was trying to find her bag at the checked baggage claim while carrying her sleeping son and a backpack. I asked her to tell me which bag was hers so I could help her get it. I pulled it off the conveyor belt and walked with her until she got outside where someone was waiting to pick her up. It took only a few minutes of my time and I was so glad I was able to help. Think of situations like that in your own life–ones where you have received help or ones where you wish you'd had help–and look for ways you can lighten someone else's load. It feels incredible!

Challenge: Choose one thing you will do to serve someone else today. Do it. Don't complicate it. Just do it.

Additional Resources:

There Is Someone Who Cares

Last week I was sitting on the couch at the end of a long day when suddenly one of my sweet sons dropped a folded up piece of paper into my lap and slipped away. I often get hand-drawn "presents" from my youngest son, but this was from one of my oldest sons and it was a complete surprise. I opened it not knowing what to expect. This is what I saw:

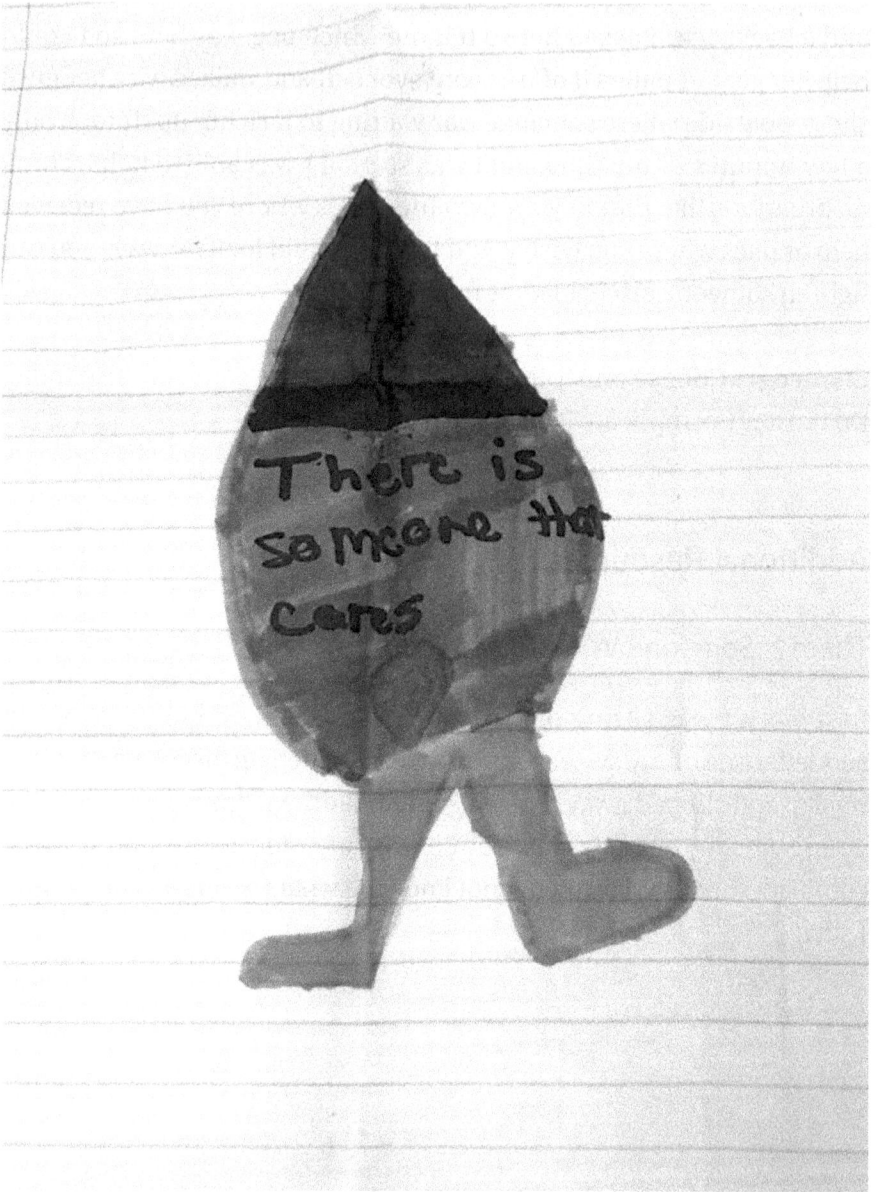

"There is someone that cares."

I couldn't help but smile at this thoughtful boy's note and I sought him out to thank him for his super kind note.

There is someone who cares.

Isn't that something we all need to hear sometimes? Just seeing those sweet words on a sheet of paper reminded me that I am not alone in all of this. So often we feel alone, don't we? We feel like no one is aware of our circumstances and no one cares. When those feelings come on, please remember that there really is someone who cares.

No man—or woman—is an island! Keeping with the geography theme and using the US as an example (since it is the geography with which I am most familiar), I find that I often feel more like Florida than Kansas. How about you?

I recently led a discussion with an awesome group of women where we talked about service. Before the day of our discussion, I had sent out an anonymous survey to this group of women asking them about ways they have helped others by serving them as well as ways others have helped them through service. The results were eye opening. Here are a few ways these women said they would like people to serve them:

Honestly sometimes a smile and friendly face is enough to brighten my day.

Just be friendly. Be a friend or a listening ear.

Have a playdate with me and my little one.

Be a friend.

Seeing their responses really opened my eyes. Sometimes I feel so overwhelmed with all that is going on in my life and I feel like I have nothing left to offer another living soul. Seeing these simple responses helped me to realize that I can offer a kind word or smile to a stranger at the grocery story or send a quick text message to a friend who comes to mind. I don't have to cook her a fancy meal or plan some elaborate get-together. I can invite someone with kids to come play with my kids.

I can LISTEN (it was my "One Little Word" in 2018...)!

Doing these small, yet meaningful services help to remind those around us that there really is someone out there who cares.

Putting the needs and wants of others ahead of ourselves is often discouraged in countless modern-day articles and speeches. We do need time to charge our own batteries–I get it. But remember balance. Remember that we are in a constant state of flux and true joy comes to our lives as we bring joy to the lives of others. The world would be a happier place if every one of us made the conscious effort to help someone today. Are you in?

We Need Each Other

I am chronically independent. To a fault. My hands can be full, my body about to topple over at any moment. yet if someone offers anything that remotely resembles help, my mouth is automatically saying, "No thanks, I'm OK," before my brain has even processed what the kind person is saying. Why do I do that?

I recently led a discussion with an incredible group of women and came to the conclusion that I am not alone in this inability to accept help, regardless of how badly I need it. One of the things that kept coming to my mind was this simple concept. I believe in God. I believe that He is all-powerful and all-knowing. I believe that He has the power to create individual planets for each and every one of us. But He didn't. On purpose. He wasn't being lazy to put us all here on this same planet. In fact, I believe He was even intentional about when and where He placed us on our shared planet. We are here–together–for very real and specific reasons.

As an introduction to our discussion, I shared pictures of different animals: fish, birds, elephants, mustangs, wolves, lions, giraffes, butterflies, wildebeasts, penguins, cows, and sheep. All of these animals thrive in groups. They vary in size and habitat, but their need for each other remains.

Then I shared a photo of a grove of trees. Henry D. Taylor shares this:

> *The story is told of a young boy who visited his uncle, a lumberjack. AT the lumber camp, the boy saw a massive tree standing alone on the top of a hill. He enthusiastically pointed the tree out to his uncle, saying, "Look at that big tree! It will make a lot of good lumber, won't it?*
>
> *His uncle looked down at the boy and shook his head. "No, son, that tree will not make a lot of good lumber. It might make a lot of lumber but not a lot of good lumber. When a tree grows off by itself, too many branches grow on it. Those branches produce knots when the tree is cut into lumber. The best lumber comes from trees that grow together in groves. The trees also grow taller and straighter when they grown together.*

And so it is with us. If we truly want to be the best that we can be, we cannot do it alone. We need each other.

To Thine Own Self Be True

I have heard the age-old argument from Shakespeare himself:

> *This above all: to thine own self be true,*
> *And it must follow, as the night the day,*
> *Thou canst not then be false to any man.*

Sure, the concept of being true to yourself is absolutely valid. But we are forgetting the rest of the advice. "Thou canst not then be false to any man [or woman]." We must not only be true to ourselves, but true to one another.

And the truth is, we are stronger, happier, and better when we give and receive help among each other. John Whittier penned one of those timeless gems of wisdom when he wrote:

Thee lift me, and I'll lift thee
  And we'll both ascend together.

I know that there are major reasons we fear reaching out to and relying on others. And those reasons are often real and slightly paralyzing.

They All Stem From Fear

Often we are afraid that if we put ourselves out there, and share our vulnerabilities with others, our hearts will be broken as a result. And that fear of a potential broken heart paralyzes us into inaction. When I was trying to decide if I wanted to date a certain boy in college more seriously, I pictured the possibility of our relationship coming to an end. I decided that we had such a great time together that even if it ended in heartbreak, it would be worth it in the end. I moved forward. Nearly 18 years later, I do not regret that decision for one minute as we continue living and loving one another side-by-side. I would never know such joy if I hadn't consciously decided to open my heart in the first place.

But it doesn't always work out that way, does it? I have given my all to friends who have moved on anyway. It hurts. I have trusted people who turned out to not be who I thought they were.

A Current Example

Within the past hour I have received two messages from two different friends. The first was a request for me to help her get her kids safely to someone who would be picking them up from school. I quickly replied that I'd be happy to help. The second was from a friend I was counting on this weekend who forgot to tell me she wasn't going to be there after all. I was crushed. I sent back a nice "Oh! OK. Have a great weekend…" sort of message and then took a minute to cry. I was really counting on her. But do you want to know what I did next? I reached out to a couple friends. I told them of my situation and how bummed out I was. I told them I was nervous and asked them to pray for me. And those friends were reassuring and supportive. One friend (my husband) even brought me a pantry-size container of Peanut M&Ms!

Sometimes people will disappoint us and hurt us. Sometimes it will be accidental and sometimes it will be intentional. This does not negate the importance of reciprocal friendship, support, and companionship. In her book Bird by Bird, Anne Lamott is introspectively considering her innate reaction to life's challenges when she observes,

"... I automatically think that closing down is safe, but ...really staying open and loving is safer, because then we're connected to all that life and love."

Marjorie P. Hinckley was one of those women who lit up a room with her humble love. I own a few books that contain her inspiring writing and each time I read them, my heart smiles. In her nineties she wisely said,

> *"Oh, how we need each other. Those of us who are old need you who are young. And, hopefully, you who are young need some of us who are old. It is a sociological fact that women need women. We need deep and satisfying and loyal friendships with each other."*

As someone who is not quite "young" anymore and not quite "old" yet (depending on whom you ask...), I see the wisdom in these words. I wish I would have started trying to apply this principle earlier in my life.

My dear friends, please never remain in loneliness. You are not alone. You were never meant to be alone. Reach out. Give help. Accept help. Together we will experience greater joy than we ever could alone. Don't deny yourself joy because of fear.

6

DON'T JUDGE

W e are so quick to judge others, especially those who make decisions different from our own. Especially when we are uncomfortable with our own choices. Haven't you recognized that those meanies that go around laughing at other people are actually the most insecure of the bunch? For the first several years of our marriage, we were not able to have children. It was painful for me and I felt very insecure around other women who had already begun their families. At the same time, when I was alone with my husband, I found myself naively judging those young mothers. Regrettable phrases like, "I can't believe she..." or "If those were my kids..." rolled from my tongue as if I had any idea what I was talking about. I didn't. In fact, even now as a mother of five kids, I still don't. I cringe now even admitting that I was so judgmental. In my mind, those women were judging me, thinking I was intentionally waiting to have children so in some silly, twisted way, I felt justified. I was wrong. Judging them did not leave me feeling justified, instead it robbed me of opportunities to feel more joy.

Do you want to know what cured me?

I got judged. Painfully and publicly by a stranger (You can read the whole story in the additional resources that follow in this chapter.). For weeks—even months—later, the words of that stranger haunted me. The experience completely changed my perspective and helped me to realize how bad it hurts to have someone judge me wrongfully and assume the worst of me. I would never wish to inflict that pain on another person.

Ann Voskamp says,

> "I won't judge you for dishes in your sink and shoes over your floor and laundry on your couch. I won't judge you for choosing not to spend your one life weeding the garden or washing the windows or working on organizing the pantry. I won't judge you for the size of your waist, the flatness, bigness, cut or color of your hair, the hipness or the matronliness of your clothes, and I won't judge whether you work at a stove, a screen, a store, a steering wheel, a sink or a stage. I won't judge you for where you are on your road, won't belittle your offering, your creativity, your battle, your work."

Let this be our motto, too. Letting go of judgment and freely giving grace to our fellow humans, is opening the windows to air out our souls and allow fresh air and light to shine in every corner. It truly brings more joy into our lives.

Challenge: The next time you think something judgmental, stop and say out loud, "I don't know what she (or he or they) is (or are) going through. I hope she is OK." and mean it.

Additional Resources:

Stop Judging!

I recently read the book *Business Boutique* by Christy Wright because I have quickly come to understand that while I know proper grammar and my spelling is pretty good, there are a lot of things about the business side of writing that I was clueless about. I am still learning. At the end of her book, she talks directly to women about creating their own versions of balance. What feels and looks balanced to you may not feel and look balanced to me and vice versa. Her words really resonated with me. She went on to talk about the plague of womanhood: judging. It's a pandemic, isn't it? It is crippling to women because it divides us and reduces our abilities to do good in this world. We are so much stronger together!

Christy says, "Often, the reason we're so quick to judge another woman with decisions different from our own is that we aren't completely comfortable with our own choices." YES! This is SO TRUE! It reminds me of how we teach our children that bullies make fun of other people because they are insecure themselves. For the first 6 years of our marriage we were not able to have children. It was painful for me and I felt very insecure around other women my age who had already begun their families. At the same time, when I was alone with my husband, I found myself naively judging those young mothers' decisions and regrettable phrases like, "I can't believe she..." or "If those were my kids..." rolled from my tongue freely. I cringe now even typing that. In my mind, those women were judging me, thinking I was intentionally waiting to have children, so I felt justified. (Pause here for a major eye roll and sigh of disgust.) Do you want to know what cured me?

I got judged. Painfully and publicly by a stranger. It completely opened my eyes.

We were flying home from a visit with my family for Christmas. It was too expensive to fly into South Carolina (where they live), so we flew into Atlanta and drove the four hours to my mom's house. Our flight from Houston to Atlanta was relatively uneventful. On the way back to Atlanta to catch our flight home to Houston, we left with plenty of time. We did not want to be late for our flight and—tiny detail here—we were traveling with three kids under the age of 2. Not an easy feat. Sadly, about an hour outside of Atlanta, we came to a complete stop on the freeway. It became a parking lot. We had three very unhappy babies in my brother's truck with us as we sat parked on the freeway for over an hour. Traffic was slow to resume moving once it did and by the time we passed the HAZMAT trucks on the shoulder, it was time for us to already be at the airport.

We called the airline over and over, but it was Christmastime and no one ever answered. By the time we arrived at the airport, we were too late. We were told that they would put us on standby and we should wait at a particular gate to see if we could get on a subsequent flight. We waited all day. Finally, as the last flight boarded that night, someone at the desk told us that one seat from our party would be able to get on that flight: my 7-month-old son! Obviously, that wasn't going to happen! So, at 9:30pm, they told us that they could definitely board us on the first flight the next morning. We got a hotel room at the airport hotel and waited for over an hour for a crib to lay our exhausted babies down.

I felt as though I had just laid my head on the pillow when it was time to get up and start the madness all over again. We loaded everyone up and did the best we could with what was left of our carry-on supplies for our three babies. We had not planned for any of this! We got back to the gate and were told that they could get all of us on the flight, but none of the seats were together, so we would have to board and then see if people would trade with us. While we were trying to collapse our stroller by the door of the plane, one of our 22-month-old twins was stumbling around and fell. He bumped his head hard enough to cry–no blood/no bruise. My husband, Nick, and I both sighed and he took the crying twin and I took the other twin and the 7-month-old with me.

Fortunately people were gracious enough to move on the plane so that I could be with two of the kids and Nick and our son who was calming down were in the very back of the plane, but at least they were together. Take-off was rough. The twin that I had is pretty high-strung and he was very nervous already and just as I gave him a pacifier to help with take-off, he dropped it and that mean old thing rolled away and was lost forever. I searched for a replacement, but couldn't find one. I bribed him with fruit snacks. I whispered prayers in his ear. I begged him to calm down. I sang whisper songs in his ear. Meanwhile, our 7-month-old was confined to his car seat and was NOT happy. I had to figure out a way to nurse him while making sure my other son was OK. It was exhausting.

Sitting across the aisle from us were two older kids (probably 7 and 10). Their mom was behind them and their dad was behind us (they were probably displaced because of us). In front of those kids was a man in his early thirties who wore an eye mask over his eyes for most of the flight and kept to himself. As we were making our descent to land in Houston, this man removed his eye mask, turned to me, and gave me a lecture that could have been entitled, "10 Reasons Why Babies Cry" after which he said that he worked at a pediatrician's office in Houston and he had never seen such a bad mother as he saw in me that day.

I was stunned. Who was this man? He didn't know me! He didn't know all of the good things I did for my children and how much I love them. He judged me and my ability to mother based on a horrible two-hour flight and not even based on what he saw, but what he'd heard. It stung. I clenched my jaw and waited for him to finish. While he was talking, I had already decided that I would not retaliate, but that I would respond with as much kindness as I could muster and hoped that would put an end to the whole thing. I simply said, "Sir, you have no idea what we have been through in the past 24 hours. I apologize for disturbing you." The father sitting behind me leaned over the seat and said, "Just wanted you to know, that guy was way out of line." Even though I appreciated his comment, in my mind I was thinking, "Everybody heard that?! Aaaahh!" As everyone else was getting off the plane, I stayed right there in my seat with my two babies, on the verge of tears as I waited for my husband to come from the very back of the plane. I felt so horrible!

For weeks after this incident, I found those words coming back to my mind and those same feelings of being judged by this ignorant man returned. How dare he? He doesn't even know me! And suddenly the words of a scripture came to my mind, "Judge not, that ye be not judged" (Matthew 7:1). Ouch. I got the message loud and clear:I knew how it felt to have someone judge me wrongfully and assume the worst of me and it felt horrible. Knowing that, how could I ever do that to someone else again? Now anytime that I start to allow my thoughts to go in that direction, I am reminded of this experience. I remember how it feels to be judged and I never wish that on another person.

Christy Wright continues her thoughts by saying, "And really, at our core, all the women I've ever met want the same things. We want a purpose we can be proud of. We want a family that is healthy and happy. We want a body that we can feel comfortable in. We want a life that we love. These are the ties that bind us together as women...Her methods may be her way and not my way, but that's okay, because it's her life. We don't need more standards to meet; we need support. We don't need more advice; we need affirmation. We don't need more guidance; we need grace."

Let's give ourselves grace. Let's give our fellow brothers and sisters grace. Ann Voskamp says,

"I won't judge you for dishes in your sink and shoes over your floor and laundry on your couch. I won't judge you for choosing not to spend your one life weeding the garden or washing the windows or working on organizing the pantry. I won't judge you for the size of your waist, the flatness, bigness, cut or color of your hair, the hipness or the matronliness of your clothes, and I won't judge whether you work at a stove, a screen, a store, a steering wheel, a sink or a stage. I won't judge you for where you are on your road, won't belittle your offering, your creativity, your battle, your work."

An Open Letter to Mothers

Dear Moms,

Remember how you were recently stressing about a decision you made, wondering if it was the best thing for your child? Remember that guilt you felt because you wished you had done better than you think you did? Remember the chore that went undone because you were too busy helping your child with something else? If so, read on—you are not alone.

Take a deep breath. You don't breathe enough. Give yourself some credit. You are doing the best you can. When you make mistakes, you are teaching your child that nobody's perfect. Don't feel guilty about your imperfections, just show your child what you are doing to make the most of them. The next time you look at someone else's life and think you are doing it all wrong, remember that you are enough. You are the person your child needs. Don't give up. Don't believe the lie. You are enough. You are not perfect, but neither is she (yeah, you know the one you keep comparing yourself to...) or anybody else. The world is a beautiful, imperfect place.

Remember that you don't have to look like someone else or do the things that someone else does. You are you for a reason. You were created and equipped specifically for your child. Your child is your child for very real reasons. Instead of listening to that negative voice that tells you falsehoods about how inadequate and inept you are, listen to that pure intuition deep in your soul that will direct you to be the very best mother you can be.

I recently came across a timely quote: "Children are tyrants. They contradict their parents, gobble their food, and tyrannize their teachers." This sounds like it came from a recent news article, right? In fact, it is from Socrates! He said this over 2000 years ago! We will spend our entire lives trying to find the best ways to meet our children's needs and to help shape them into happy, successful, well-adjusted adults, but in the meantime, we will often feel like failures. This is not unique

46

to us. This is a universal, age-old truth.

In the 1600s, a man named John Wilmot wrote, "Before I got married, I had six theories about bringing up children. Now I have six children and no theories." Sound familiar? Sister, you are not alone.

Remember that friend who was seemingly bragging to you about her child and her recent accomplishments? She wasn't trying to make you feel even more inadequate, she was just searching for some sort of validation. Being a mother is a lot like working as a top-secret spy: you often can't talk about exactly what it is you do every day, and even if you could, nobody else would understand anyway. No one else can do your job quite the way you can. Keep working!

The next time you are feeling discouraged and believe yourself to be a complete failure (because we all do sometimes), focus on progress instead of perfection. None of us humans is perfect. Just keep moving forward. It may be centimeters, it may me miles, just keep going. Each day, each year, will bring different challenges and different opportunities. Focus on progress. If you fall backwards a little in one area, consider how you can adjust and move forward again. Imagine you are in a car, driving up a steep hill. If you put your car in neutral halfway up the hill, will it continue to go up? No! It will speed back down. Now you are back at the bottom, but you can still get over this steep hill if you will just stay in the car, keep it in drive and keep moving in the right direction. It may slow down at the steepest points, but you will get there if you keep inching forward.

We live in a society that seeks to shame and demean mothers. Many "experts" claim to have all the answers and if we try to follow our own intuition with our own children, we often feel judged and even condemned. Don't let the ignorance of others desensitize you! You are powerful beyond measure and you are a light to your children. Let that power and light thrive within your home, regardless of the opinions of others. Make educated decisions for your family based on your family's needs and your intuition and do not worry if your decision is not a duplicate of what it seems "everyone else" is doing. And, while you're at it, cut those other mothers some slack, too, so they can do what is right for their families. Nobody wants to feel judged.

Whether you read this in the morning or at night, in January or October, know that you can start (or restart) NOW. You don't have to wait and you are not too late. You are enough. You are not perfect, but you are enough. You can do your best and that best will be exactly what your child needs. Let your calming, deep breaths be the wind beneath your child's wings. You can do this!

Sincerely,

Your sister and friend

Kindness

I recently read an inspiring article about **kindness** written by Barbara A. Lewis. I highlighted three profound sentences that I want to share with you:

> *"A lack of kindness can begin with critical thoughts of others, and it can develop into a habit of finding fault. However, if we accept responsibility for our own reactive thinking, we can become more charitable. Rather than judging others, we grow in understanding, and kindness."*

I have been thinking about this concept since I read her article and how true her statement is. How many times have you had a strained relationship with someone that began with critical thoughts?

"Why doesn't he _____?"

"Why does she always _____?"

"He shouldn't _____."

"She should have _____."

Our negativity and our unkind actions only grow from there. Since these critical thoughts are the root of our problem, what can we do to change this habit?

Someone once told me, "We judge others by their perceived actions. We judge ourselves by our intentions."

This is so true and so unfair! We have no idea what another person's intentions are because we are not that person. When we let those critical thoughts based on perceived actions take root in our hearts, they continue to grow and develop into habits of fault-finding.

"So what can we do instead?"

We can be intentional with our thoughts. When a critical thought comes to our minds, we can give others the grace we hope they would give us. We can LET IT GO. Fortunately, we are not omniscient beings who hold the responsibility to judge everyone in every situation and decide who is right and who is wrong. Instead of focusing our energy on criticism and judging and fault-finding, we can use that energy to remind us that we never have the whole picture because we are limited by our own limitations and perspectives. Yes, you may feel your way of thinking is superior and absolute, but it is possible the other person feels the exact same way about his own way of thinking.

"But I'm just trying to help!"

Are you? Is this like how my son said he "accidentally" stepped on his brother? Sometimes we would do ourselves a lot of good if we stopped ourselves in the middle of a critical thought and asked,

"Why am I thinking about this?"

Since I recently read *Ramona Quimby, Age 8* with my boys for their summer reading, this quote about Ramona from the end of the book comes to my mind:

> *"Deep down inside, she felt she herself was nice all the time, but sometimes on the outside her niceness sort of—well, curdled. Then people did not understand how nice she really was. Maybe other people curdled too."*

Just as Lewis states in her article, we will grow in understanding and kindness when we intentionally refrain from judging others or criticizing them. We may regret unkind words that come up from our hearts, through our mouth, and out into the air, but we will undoubtedly never regret kindnesses shown to others whether known or unknown. I think we can all benefit from being a bit kinder, don't you?

7

BE GRATEFUL

S ometimes burdens and frustrations become so heavy that they are all we can think about–I get it. We've all been there. But when we can't see the forest for the trees, we need to back up and change our perspective.

Think of all of that is good right now.

Let's start with three things that you are grateful for right now.

1-

2-

3-

Did any of those make you grin a little? I hope so! Now let's add a few more. Think of a person in your life you are grateful for (past or present). What did that person do for you? Think of a talent or strength you have (yes, you have at least one...). Think of your favorite food. Think of your favorite flower/plant/tree. Think of that miraculous event that happened in your life that you still can't explain as anything but a miracle.

Your heart is beating.

You are breathing.

These mean you have opportunity.

Taking a few moments to practice gratitude is empowering. It reminds us that joy already exists in our lives, we just have to choose to let *it* be the driving force instead of those negative looming emotions.

Your heart wants to be joyful—let it! Release those heavy emotions and allow joy to fill your heart as you consider all of the gifts you have been given in your life. No, your life is not perfect. No one's life is perfect! There is no human being on the planet who is living a perfect life no matter what your social media feeds say to the contrary!

While you are waiting in a LONG checkout line, or on hold, or in the carpool line at your kids' school, allow your mind to focus on those things that you are most grateful for. Consider the beauty all around you. Consider the love all around you. Consider the goodness all around you. Remember that shadows are simply evidence of light. Focus on the light. Celebrate it in all its forms. This celebration of light is joy.

Challenge: Make a list of 100 things you are grateful for. Ready? Go!

Additional Resources:

Grateful for Growth

I love to hike. Have you ever noticed, though, that the most beautiful vistas always seem to follow the toughest hikes? I have yet to travel on easy, flat terrain that has led me a short distance to a jaw-dropping view. No, it always comes after effort, often some time, and many times steep inclines and switchbacks. I usually want to give up before I get there. When I reach the end of the trail, however, I am so grateful that I didn't give up because the final destination is always better than I'd imagined.

I have so many things in my life to be grateful for. A few weeks ago I had the opportunity to spend several hours in Denver. I walked around downtown exploring and even got a haircut! As I talked with the girl who cut my hair, she repeated back to me what I had just told her, "So you write children's books, teach a few English classes online and get to spend the day with your five beautiful children?" I smiled and affirmed that yes, that was my life. She said, "You are living the dream!" I was taken aback by this young girl's statement. My life is not glamorous or even remotely easy, but it is exactly what I want and need.

Most times when I write a list of things I am grateful for, I can go on and on for a long time thinking of all of the happy, positive things in my life. It is only when I am being truly introspective that I realize one of the biggest blessings that imposed itself on my life for nearly 6 long years: infertility.

My husband and I were married in May of 2003. Our twins—the first of our five angels—were born in 2009. That's the short version. The painless version. To be honest, though, those years were full of heartache. I prayed—begged and pleaded—to be a mother. I had decided not to pursue a full-time teaching job right out of college because I knew that I wanted to stay at home with our children and I felt that if I started teaching, I'd never want to leave. I knew I'd love it. I worked for a few years as an office manager for student housing. During that time, I met thousands of amazing people who came and went quickly because of the transient nature of student housing. I still have kind notes they have written me and fond memories in my heart of the many people I met during that time. I learned a lot about the kind of mother I wanted to be (and the kind of mother I didn't want to be).

By the time my husband graduated and we moved to Houston, I had already attended at least 50 baby showers (it felt like 500) for other expectant mothers and I cried at nights wishing it could be my turn to hold up the cute onesies and receiving blankets. I thought I was ready to be a mother. I decided to stop attending baby showers.

We signed a four month lease for an apartment in Houston while we searched for our first home to purchase. We were still hopeful that miracles would happen and children would join our family. Plus, we were both so tired of living in apartments with shared walls and distant parking. We were ready to settle in to our own home, even if we didn't "need" it yet. So in November of 2006, we bought our first house. It is the home we are still living in today.

For the first year that we lived there, the house looked much like I felt: empty. I started to think that this miracle I had wanted my entire life would never happen. I served in church, worked a random job at a scrapbooking store and sought out doctors from any friend who would recommend one to find out what was wrong with me. It was a painful time. We got a puppy, trying to fill the empty void that was gnawing at my insides.

It was like my heart was hungry. I couldn't ignore it and those hunger pangs were constant. I was so blessed during that time to meet more amazing friends in the scrapbooking industry and a very dear friend who was also struggling with infertility and had been for longer than I. I clung to her and admired her strength. I am sure I sounded like an ungrateful baby to her, but I am eternally grateful for her patience with me and for her friendship. We spent tearful Mother's Days together and the four of us even went on a vacation together. As lonely and isolating as infertility can be, I felt like I had someone who could understand how I felt for the first time.

This friendship helped give me the confidence I needed to leave the little scrapbooking store job I had been hiding in and to pursue my passion of teaching. I began taking the courses to receive my Texas teachers license. A few short months later, I was shopping for a suit to wear to interviews with this friend and not long after that I landed my first teaching job: 8th grade English. I loved—and still love—being a teacher! I am so grateful for that experience. I learned so much about how to be a parent from being a teacher. I learned a lot about kids and a lot about myself. I felt fulfilled. As I came into my second year of teaching, I came to accept that if my only children were the ones I taught in my classroom each day and the ones I served through the youth program in our church, I would be grateful for those opportunities and I would stop complaining.

Soon into my second year of teaching, however, we discovered that we would be expecting twins! I will never forget the feeling that rushed over me and the instant healing I felt as I heard their heartbeats for the first time. Not surprisingly, I cried (I guess I do that a lot...), but this time I cried out of pure joy and gratitude.

Now on those toughest of days when everyone seems to be fighting or my kids seem to be intentionally pushing my every button, I remind myself, "I begged for this." And the frustration I feel may not completely disappear, but it definitely lessens. I know that motherhood is not easy, but I lived a 6-year training program that has helped me be the best mother I can be. I will never take this life of mine for granted because I am now able to "live the dream."

If I could go back in time, I would want to hug that heartbroken version of myself who still remembers what it felt like to be excused from an organized panel of leaders because I was "not a mother." I would want to assure her that those painful Mother's Day programs with adorable children singing sweet songs would not be painful forever. But, just as any metamorphosis, mine was painful out of necessity and I am the woman and the mother I am today because of those years of infertility. Because I am grateful for now, I am grateful for then because it helped me to reach this now. I am a completely different (and hopefully better) version of myself than I was back in 2003 and my children deserve that. Now that I can see the bigger picture, I realize the wisdom in my six-year struggle and I would never want to go back and erase it (though I often wish I could go back and fix my own attitude though—it wasn't pretty).

For those of you who have struggled or currently are struggling with challenges in your life, I hope you will feel the assurance that one day you will see how those challenges have helped to shape you and bring you to a better version of yourself. Our challenges are not the same because we are not the same, but the universal truth is we all have challenges. Wherever you are on your journey, I hope you will find joy and continue to trust that this challenge is not forever.

Keep hiking, friend, and be assured that you are in for some beautiful vistas when you reach the end of this trail.

Giving + Thanks: Thoughts About Giving

Maybe it's the writer in me, but I find myself thinking about individual words and their meanings quite often. Yeah, I'm OK if that officially makes me weird.

For the past few weeks I have been thinking about the word "Thanksgiving." Most of all, I have considered why this holiday is called "Thanksgiving" and not "Thanks-saying." I mean, if I'm being totally honest, our greatest attempts at expressing gratitude on Thanksgivings past have been just that: saying what we are grateful for. I even shared about my own gratitude for growth.

Don't get me wrong: we aren't apathetic to the cause. In years past, we have put in an effort toward focusing on gratitude, especially since having kids.

We have created a giant "Thankful Tree" in our hallway and had the kids fill the walls with beautiful leaves each night that contain the names of specific items for which they are thankful. I kept many of those leaves from years ago and re-read them when I pull out the Fall decorations that I put up after Halloween. I love the reminders of our blessings and the things that make me and my family happy.

I lined our Thanksgiving table with craft paper one year and encouraged all our guests to fill it with things they are thankful for.

I hang signs that say "Thankful" and "Thanks;" reminders about the meaning behind this annual national holiday and an important state of mind.

But the day—the word—isn't "Thanks-saying." It's Thanksgiving.

What does it mean to "give thanks"?

I have thought about this a lot over the past couple weeks. Obviously the key difference between the two words is in the word "giving."

The free online dictionary provides four definitions for the verb form of "give":

1-freely transfer the possession of (something) to (someone); hand over to

2-cause or allow (someone or something) to have something, especially something abstract; provide or supply with

3-carry out or perform (a specified action)

4-yield as a product or result

While saying "thank you" is a fantastic start, I don't think that it truly encompasses "giving thanks." How do you show someone that you truly appreciate an object she gave you? You use it, or put it on display, and celebrate it often. Your heart warms each time you think of the giver of said gift and you mention your gratitude often. You may even consider giving a similar gift to someone else in the future.

There is more action involved.

This year I am thinking of ways to do more giving as an expression of my gratitude instead of simple spoken words. The following is a brainstormed list of ways I came up with.

-Give heartfelt notes of appreciation to people in your life.

-Give some favorite foods to a local food bank.

-Give a phone call to someone you haven't talked to in a while.

-Give your time to help someone you care about.

-Give help to someone.

-Give a genuine compliment.

-Give a kind attitude even when things aren't going your way.

-Wish the cashier at the store "Happy Thanksgiving" and give him a smile.

-Give of your talents. If you sing, share a song. If you play an instrument, play a song. If you arrange beautiful flower arrangements, give an arrangement. If you are a good at supporting and lifting others, you guessed it: do it!

-Give the last of your patience. In that moment when you feel it wearing thin, push yourself to give more.

I know that I would feel appreciated if I received any of these in my life, so I have been trying for the past few weeks to do these things for the people in my life. I doubt it has done much in the life-changing department for anyone else.

But it has definitely done a lot for me.

Instead of just thinking about how much I appreciate other people and items in my life the way I do when I list them or say them, I feel that gratitude. Deeply. And it has brought joy and peace into my life during a crazy and hectic time. I found myself smiling and feeling hopeful even when I had little reason to do so. Please don't misinterpret this post as one of those "you're not doing enough–do more..." posts. I think that if you stop and think for a moment, you'll recognize that you have probably already done a few of the things on my list already. The main idea here is to simply continue to do them, just add some intention so that you give yourself the opportunity to feel the benefits of what you are already doing.

Gratitude is not something we can or should limit to lip service. Gratitude is something that can warm our hearts and lift our spirits, if we will let it. Gratitude will truly transform us into more joyful creatures if we will move beyond mentions and lists and push for truly giving thanks.

8

GOOD HABITS

G ood habits boost willpower. Don't we all need more willpower in our lives? Willpower is like fuel in a car. We can have our GPS on, we can even have an ultra-safe, fuel-efficient vehicle, but if we run out of gas, it is all for naught.

When we can create habits out of things that we want to be sure we do every day, we leave our willpower available for those unexpected, often inconvenient moments that arise every day. This will enable us to handle those moments without regret, allowing more joy in our lives. Regret is a big time joy-sucker! Don't let it get you!

So what can we do? Start by thinking about your day. What does an ideal day look like to you? No, I don't mean in that fantasy where you are sitting poolside all day in a cabana. I mean, on a normal (realistic) day, what are the things you want to accomplish? List them.

Now that you have your list, look over them and group them into categories by when you would like to get them done. If you have a few things that you would ideally like to get done every morning (like a load of laundry/unload the dishwasher/shower/exercise/practice an instrument), plan them into a working morning routine. Now, you are going to start with ONE. Pick ONE and focus on doing that ONE every morning for the next few weeks. Once that has become an easy part of your morning, choose the second from the list. Incorporate that into your routine and focus on maintaining your original thing plus this new

ONE thing. Keep moving forward slowly, adding one new thing at a time until you have a working routine and new habits that work for you.

Challenge: Choose the one habit you want to focus on and commit to focusing on maintaining that ONE habit for the next three weeks. Mark it on a calendar. At the end of those three weeks, reevaluate. Do you feel like it has become a habit yet? If you didn't put your energy and focus there, would you still naturally do this thing without thinking? If not, add another week of focus to the calendar. Reevaluate after a week. Some habits take longer (especially ones we don't love to do). Eventually they will stick. Just keep trying.

Additional Resources:

Want More Peace?

As I think more and more about what I do with my time, I realize the importance of habits.

Alignment

When we align our values with our habits, we will invite peace into our lives. Sure, I can type a bold statement, but what can we do with that to actually achieve it? If you really want to go there with me today, grab a pen/pencil and piece of paper (or open the "notes" app in your phone...) and keep reading.

Application

Let's start by looking at today. What does your day look like. I don't mean what is on your "to do" list, I mean what have you planned for today. Look at each of the hours in the day and identify what you did or what you have planned for today.

Now we need to talk about what is most important to you. For me, that is a sweeping statement. Where do I even begin? So let's break it down even further. What is most important to you...

...regarding your relationships?

...regarding your physical well-being?

...regarding your emotional well-being?

...regarding your financial well-being?

...regarding your employment?

Hopefully those questions got at least five things down that are MOST important to you. If you have more than 7 or 8 things, you have some that are more important, but not most—trim it down.

OK. Now look at your hours above. How many of those hours' activities were related to the things that are on your list of MOST important? Now it is time for personal reflection.

Does your schedule

reflect those things

that are most important

to you?

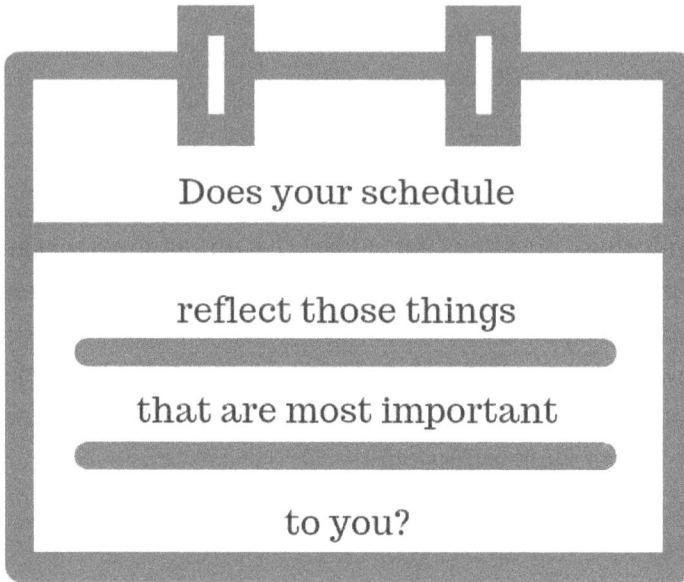

If so, great! But chances are, if you are human and still breathing right now, you have some room for improvement. Are all of your important things being addressed every day? Probably not, and that is OK, but is there a priority that you might want to focus more time and energy on tomorrow? Circle it, highlight it, or email it to yourself.

Now is the Time for Change

If your day full of activities is not reflecting your list of priorities, now is the time to make a change. Nobody can—or should—overhaul her entire schedule in one day. So today, choose ONE priority that you want to plug into your schedule. It may be your top priority or it may be the most urgent or it may be the one you know you never fit into your schedule. Put it on there—even if it's for 5:00am or 10:00pm, plan to make it a part of your day today if you can, tomorrow if your day is almost over and you can't plug it in till tomorrow. The key is to do it! Even writing it down on a schedule for tomorrow will feel so good!

Don't get tempted to change 20 things on your schedule tomorrow—that's cruel, practically impossible, and pointless. One at a time. Stick to your one thing each day for the rest of the week and then next week, you can decide if you feel ready to add a second thing. Don't rush. You are building habits here. If you try to juggle too many new things at once, they will all come toppling down and you feel like a big failure. (P.S. Everybody drops things sometimes! Don't beat yourself up, just pick them up and try again.)

Let's **not** think of this re-alignment as being like when you take your car in to get it re-aligned and they come back an hour or so later and it's all done. This re-alignment is like re-aligning teeth. As in braces for years. It is a LONG process. Teeth don't move (and stay moved) without braces and time, right? Neither do our habits. Just make one adjustment at a time and continue to check back in with yourself. Be fair and give yourself grace! Depending on the state of your teeth to begin with, the orthodontist will give you an idea of how long the treatments will take before your teeth are completely aligned. It is the same idea here. Depending on the state of your current schedule and how it aligns with your priorities, your efforts may require you to work at this for weeks or months.

Leave Guilt Behind

As you make these changes, you will notice how much easier your days become. Are they full and busy? Yes, but you will find you have more energy and you feel more peace in your life because you are not being weighed down by those persistent feelings of guilt all the time. You know what I'm talking about, don't you? You know, the guilty feelings you have that you feel you should be doing something that you just haven't gotten around to in a while, or ever. When you align your priorities and your schedule, you will feel like you are doing all the things you need to do and you will feel better about leaving some things behind. Remember: **NO ONE ON THIS PLANET CAN DO EVERYTHING**! Don't even try. Don't set yourself up for failure. Focus on your priorities and be intentional. This won't happen by accident or coincidence.

One final newsflash for today: Priorities change. We come through different seasons in our lives and what is of utmost importance to you today, may not even rank a year from now. Don't hang on to those things! Push them out of your schedule and make room for the things that are important to you right here and right now. If you notice, I have been very careful to avoid using examples in this post. Never add something to your schedule because you feel obligated to do it because other people are (or seem to be) doing it. Do what matters to you. Do what resonates with you. Trust your gut—that little voice inside will whisper and confirm that you are on the right track.

Don't trains look strange and bulky when they are just sitting on tracks and not moving? Don't lose momentum! Keep moving, even if it's slow movement. You are creating a life you love!

I hope this helps to bring more joy into your life. I want you to know that this is something I am constantly working on and thinking about in my own life, I know how daunting it can seem. You've got this!

Good Habits Boost Willpower

I have been thinking a lot lately about habits and routines. I recently read the book *Deep Work* by Cal Newport. He writes quite a bit about the value of making good habits. He quotes Pulitzer Prize-winner Robert Caro as saying, "I trained myself to be organized." I love that! I wasn't naturally an organized person and my siblings can all attest to the messiness of my bedroom throughout my childhood (Once our house was broken into and when the police came, they came into the bedroom I shared with my sister and said, "It looks like they really ransacked this room." I was so embarrassed to admit that it looked like that already.). But through that experience (and many others like it) I learned that clutter and disorganization are frustrating. Looking for things is oh-so frustrating to me. I hate to waste time hunting for something that should have been in a certain place and wasn't, don't you? So, if you feel disorganized and think it is just who you are, take heart: you can train yourself to be organized!

Start with something small like your car keys. Choose a "home" for these keys. I have a particular pocket in my purse designated as the pocket for my keys, so as soon as I leave the car, I put my keys back into that pocket. Then when I have to go somewhere, the keys are already in that pocket. Choose the home for your keys and then practice **only** this one thing for a few weeks. When you are no longer hunting for your keys and have them always where you want them, you are ready to move on to another item in your life. Don't try to wake up next Monday and "be organized." That isn't how it works. When you train for a marathon, or train for a spelling bee, or when your little girl is potty-training, or when you train for anything, you must practice a little at a time until you build yourself up to where you want to be.

In *Deep Work*, Newport also refers to a 2012 study led by two psychologists Wilhelm Hofmann and Roy Baumeister. They studied adults, recording their feelings at random intervals throughout each day. After one week, the researchers gathered more than 7500 samples and, in short, they found that "people fight desires all day long."

Newport writes that Roy Baumeister continued his studies and learned another profound truth, this time about our individual willpower:

"You have a finite amount of willpower that becomes depleted as you use it."

Cal Newport compares willpower to a muscle—it can become tired and worn out after extensive use. This is why habits are so important. Making things we value habitual in our lives helps preserve our willpower for the unexpected. If we are using all our willpower each day just to force ourselves to do the things we know we should be doing anyway, when problems arise or our children fight more than usual or our favorite store has a big sale or a friend calls to gossip, we have no willpower left to react the way we wish we could. But if we have made habits out of those things we value more, we are saving our finite willpower for those hectic times that arise every—single—day.

Personally, this research sheds light on why bedtime is such a hectic and often miserable/challenging/frustrating time for all parties involved! My willpower has been completely used up and my children's willpower evaporated hours ago and now here we are, all willpower-less trying to coexist and it is a struggle! They know that they should not be running through the house naked playing tag and fighting and climbing walls and throwing water out of the shower and standing on the toilet and squirting toothpaste on the bathroom mirror and yelling and throwing toys down the stairs but they have been going strong all day and their willpower is gone. I know that I shouldn't get angry because they are just kids and they are learning from my example and they are exhausted, yet my depleted willpower at night prevents me from such logical thinking and often I find myself just trying to muster up one more minute of strength to breath deeply and not completely explode amid all the chaos.

When I was a young girl, I ran on a track team for a couple of years. I usually ran the mile at each meet; I even won a few times. One thing that I have always remembered from that time is the idea that I had to set a pace for myself and try to maintain that pace throughout the race, but when the final lap came, it was time to push. I had to push myself as hard as I could and go faster than I realized I could, mustering energy I didn't realize I still had to win the race.

Now as a mom processing this concept, I realize that I must utilize this skill with my willpower. Each day is another race in the sense that I need to set a pace throughout the day that will keep my willpower usage at manageable levels so that at the end of the day I will be able to access that reserve of energy and push through any exhaustion I may be feeling. I don't want to just survive each night. My time with my children is limited. I want to win. I want to walk out of their bedrooms when I turn off the lights and feel success and not regret. I know that challenges arise and **no** day will be perfect (you hear that perfectionists out there—**NO** day is perfect!), but I can give it my best and learn from my mistakes and keep working.

Habits are a highly personal thing. The habits I want to have and habits I want to break are likely different from the habits you want and don't want, so I will not waste our time prescribing what habits you should make or what habits you should break. I will just offer you these thoughts and encourage you to start today with one. Choose a small habit you want to start whether it's keeping your kitchen sink clean, writing 1000 words per day, reading scripture, running, a workout program, using a planner, or something completely different—do it. Start today. Then give yourself grace because you are investing in your future with the work you are putting into today's habit. Habits don't form overnight, but they do start with one day. Let's get started!

9

INSPIRING WORDS

You know the old saying, "Sticks and stones may break my bones, but words will never hurt me." It's false. Words can hurt us. They do all the time. But words can also inspire us. Words are powerful things. The words we choose to surround ourselves with can be extremely influential on our joy. Choose wisely.

Look for quotes and messages that inspire you and lift you up and put them in places where you will see them and find them when you need them. I keep a Pinterest board full of inspiring words (come on over and follow it—I add new inspiration all the time!). I hang important and inspiring words on the walls in every room of our house.

Intentionally search for words that inspire you and that resonate with you. These may be in the form of scriptures. Read them regularly. I spend time at the beginning of each day reading scripture. Our days always go better when we start with some inspiring words.

Challenge: Find a quote/scripture that inspires you. Write it out or print it and hang it in a prominent place where you will see it often.

Additional Resources:

Words are Powerful Things

I confess: I love words. I love to read them, listen to them, speak them, and especially write them. I love the power that words carry. You know the old saying, "Sticks and stones can break my bones but words will never hurt me"? It's false. I don't even bother teaching this lie to my kids. Words hurt. In fact, on the wall in our playroom, we've hung a few different quotes:

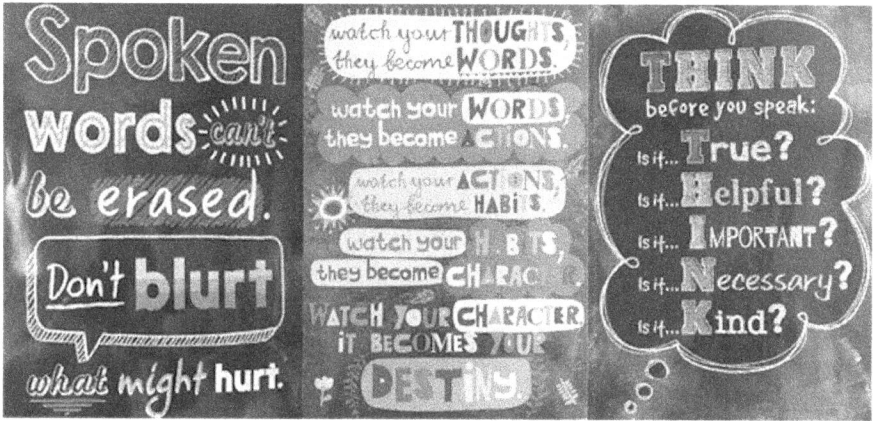

Words can inspire us, words can hurt us, words can make us laugh, words can make us cry, words teach us. I marvel at the power that these combinations of letters have. Since my One Little Word of 2018 was LISTEN, I have paid particular attention to the words that come from other people and I see how those words affect me and others as well.

As I started putting this post together, I realized that I have quotes and inspiring words all around me. Just beside my desk on the wall of my office, I have taped FOUR quotes! Here is one of them from Neal A. Maxwell:

"Not shrinking is more important than surviving."

When our boys were babies, I made decorations for their nursery wall that donned the words:

> *"Learn what you should learn. Do what you should do. Be what you should be."*

I line our shelves with books full of words: some inspiring, some entertaining, some funny, some scary, some educational. I even have words in vinyl on our kitchen wall that have been there now for over a decade!

Even the home page of my website (alimcjoy.com) includes three of my all-time favorite quotes! Words are a huge part of my life and I am sure that they are a huge part of your life, too. The words we choose to surround ourselves with can either empower us or stress us out. It is our choice.

Pinterest

I have been teaching English classes in some form for quite a while. When I taught in public school settings both in middle school and community college, I always began my classes with a Quote of the Day journaling prompt. I encouraged my students to write about the quote each day and to apply it to specific experiences in their own lives. We would then take a few minutes to share some of our responses and thoughts before we continued on with the rest of the day's work. It was one of my favorite things and even my more resistant writers came to enjoy it. Several years ago, I began collecting more quotes to use in my classes, so I created a Pinterest page just for such quotes. If you need some inspiring words in your life, feel free to visit or follow my Pinterest page.

The Power of One Little Word

{This is from a post I wrote at the end of December 2017. I hope my thoughts will inspire you to consider the power of words in your life.}

For several years now I have followed Ali Edwards and have loved her idea of focusing on "One Little Word" instead of a long list of resolutions. Her idea was intriguing, and for the first few years, I mused over what my "One Little Word" would be, but I didn't really do anything with it. I didn't commit.

For the past several years, however, I have committed myself to this idea of "One Little Word." I have loved seeing these words come into my life and help shape me into a better version of myself. Each year, I think I have an idea of how that word will change me, but at the end of that year I am always surprised at how I see and understand the word in completely different ways. I love it! In the past I have chosen the words prosper, open, together, and forward.

In 2017, I chose a word that scared me quite a bit. I didn't advertise that this was my word because I thought it would defeat the purpose of my word, but now as my year is coming to a close, I have come to understand this word so much better and I realize that my word has really pushed me to do a lot things that were not comfortable this year.

So, in the spirit of discomfort and acceptance, I will tell you that my word for 2017 was MEEK. When I began the year, I thought that this word would lead to a really quiet year for me where most of my roles would be behind-the-scenes, supporting others. I thought that was what meekness was.

I did enjoy quite a bit of that this year, but I also came to realize that I was allowing my pride to stop me from trying new things. I love to write and I have always written, but I was afraid that people wouldn't want to read what I wrote or that it would be too boring or unsophisticated and I would just embarrass myself. My silly pride let me believe that if I never shared what I wrote, I could believe that I was good and no one could argue otherwise. As I focused on trying to incorporate more meekness in my life this year, I realized that I needed to let go of my pride and allow myself to learn and make mistakes and try publicly. I have things to share and unique perspectives that can make the world a better place (you do, too, by the way) and—at least to me—part of being meek is being willing to share those freely without accolades. So I self-published a book, then I built my own website and started a blog. Then I went about learning from the mistakes of my first book and wrote and published a second book. I have learned so much this year and feel so excited for the progress I have made. I never expected any of this to come from meekness!

I usually start thinking of my new word in November, so that I can narrow it down, pray about it, talk it over with my husband, and prepare myself for January. Want to know my new word for 2018? It's LISTEN.

This word scares me a little, too! I know that much learning comes from listening and I look forward to learning so much more this year. I also know that relationships are strengthened from listening, so I am excited to see how my relationships evolve this year. While I try really hard to be a good listener, I fear that I often fail at this. I interrupt people when they are talking, I shush my kids when they are talking too loudly—often before I even know what they were trying to communicate—, I sometimes smile and laugh in a conversation even if I haven't quite heard what was actually said (sorry, friends!). I have some improving to do, for sure! I am also VERY visual! If I really want to get information, I read it because I can comprehend and internalize it so much better that way. I occasionally listen to an audiobook, but I prefer reading the book because I can remember and understand more when I can see the words on the page. In my book Picky I talk about the importance of listening to your body, particularly when it comes to eating. I think I will need to do a better job this year of listening to my body and resting when I need to rest and eating/drinking when I need to. I often work right through a lunch or I postpone breakfast so I can eek out a couple more paragraphs before my writing time is over. As I was working hard to get my *Oggie the Otter* book out before

December, I was so uptight, I could barely turn my head! My neck and shoulders were so tense it was causing me physical pain. I need to do better about listening to my body and my mind and not get so stressed out, particularly over things that are beyond my control.

10

BALANCE

B alance is not a destination we can reach. Balance is a constant movement, shifting and changing with each situation. In order to maintain balance, we cannot stay in the same place, but must be constantly adjusting.

This means if you are still trying to maintain the same morning routine you had a few years ago, you may need to take some time to rethink that. Have your circumstances changed? Are you in a different season of life now than you were a few years ago? If so, your morning routine will need to adjust to create a new balance.

Day-to-day adjustments may need to be made as well. For example, if your regular routines call for an early wake-up time, you may need to give yourself some grace and have a contingency plan for those days when you wake up with a child having a bathroom emergency at 2am. That is true balance. Those feelings of balance will help you to be able to see and feel the joy in your life.

Challenge: What does balance look like in your current season of life? To get there, consider what an ideal day would look like (you know, in that imaginary perfect world we all dream about).

If adjustments need to be made to your daily routines, choose ONE adjustment to make today and get started.

Additional Resources:

The Myth of Balance

Did you ever dream of finding a pot of gold at the end of a rainbow? I did. If you (like me) tried to find this mythical pot of gold, you may have noticed that the "end" of the rainbow seems attainable until you approach it, and then it seems ever-elusive or just disappears. Through the beauty of science, we can know that a rainbow is actually a complete circle, thus having no beginning and no end—no place for a pot of gold to exist.

More often then not when I talk with others about life struggles, I find that we have replaced the rainbow myth with a new, more "grown-up" myth: *balance*. Now before you shut down on me or go off on me (or both...), hear me out. I do not think that *balance* is actually a myth. The problem is, we are seeing balance incorrectly, just like when we look for an end to a rainbow. We think that balance is some form of quiet stasis that we can attain and everything will be right with the world (our pot of gold). *This* is the myth.

In reality, balance is a constant flux. Balance, much like the circle of water droplets reflecting light we call a rainbow, is conditional. Balance shifts and changes with each situation. Balance requires constant adjustment in order to be maintained. My favorite example of what balance really looks like can be found in a YouTube video.

The video shows a woman named Faith Dickey from the United States (the state of Texas) who is in Croatia to perform an amazing stunt. Faith balances on a rope strung across a median between two trucks driving side-by-side down both sides of an empty highway at speeds of about 50mph. And if that isn't challenging enough, the timing is limited by two tunnels in the distance. She must walk from one truck across the rope to the other truck before they arrive at the entrances to the tunnels and the rope snaps. It is an intense stunt.

In a subsequent interview with Faith, she shares some of her secrets for this amazing feat. "You have to keep your back really straight," she says, "This is really important 'cause it helps center your weight over the line. You also want your feet to be in the same direction as the line — so walking forwards, not to the side. Not only that, but your arms are always in the air. Those are acting as your balancing pole. So when your weight shifts one way, you want to counteract that by throwing your arms to the other side."

Constant adjustment in action.

So what do you do to find and maintain balance between two trucks moving at 50 miles per hour?

Faith replies, "There was a really strong wind coming from this side, so it felt like it was pushing me over this way. So I was trying to stay really straight and lean against the wind a little bit — so that I kept my body straight rather than falling off in that direction. Not only that, but I wasn't the one shaking the line...It was the trucks and the road. It would shake without me knowing where the shake was coming from and I had to adjust really quickly."

Experts say that what makes this trick work is something called frames of reference. The trucks are moving at the same speed and so is Faith. So technically, it's just like doing this trick in a parking lot, only with howling winds. The trick, according to Faith, is constant adjustment.

Balance IRL

Maybe you have already accepted that balance requires constant adjustment. Maybe you rolled your eyes at my statement about balance being a form of stasis. That's cool. But maybe your idea of balance was from the idea of a tightrope walker on a circus stage. Their adjustments and corrections are barely discernible as they maintain their steady pace from point A to point B. *This*, you've thought to yourself, *is what balance is. This is what I want.*

But let's be real. We are never on an empty stage, only seeking to balance across two fixed points with lovely background music to help us maintain our focus. We don't have the luxury of putting all our energy on just one element, our hands free to hold a balance beam. No, typically we are trying to maintain — or establish — balance while 5,472,936, other things are going on all around us, our hands too full to even consider carrying a balance beam. Like Faith Dickey's balancing act across the trucks, we must constantly adjust in order to make it to our "point B" before we smash into the wall of an upcoming tunnel.

This is where we can see that Faith Dickey's constant adjustments and recoveries are crucial in order to achieve any sort of lasting balance in our own intense stunts — I mean, lives.

Falling is Inevitable

When Faith begins her stunt, she slips. Fortunately, she grabs the rope, pulls herself back up and keeps going. This was her first attempt at a stunt like this. It was inevitable. The next time we try something new and we fall, we can remember that balance can still be found. We can get up and try again. We will lean into the wind next time instead of letting it knock us down. We will constantly adjust.

In our day-to-day challenges to achieve balance, Faith's example is so very pertinent: we must walk forward, stand straight, and constantly adjust. If we do, we will progress. We will eventually make it to where we want to be. Constant adjustment is balance.

11

FINAL THOUGHTS

Whether you are finishing this book for the first time or the eleventh time, I hope that it has brought more joy to your life. I hope that you are feeling that lasting combination of elation and peace. Hold on to it and don't let go! Keep seeking joy.

I would be remiss if I did not share with you that the greatest source of joy in my life has come through my relationship with my loving Heavenly Father and my Savior Jesus Christ. I know that not everyone shares this same faith and I am not a judge in any sense of the word, so your personal faith is just that: personal. But since I have shared with you ten ways to increase the joy in your life, I feel I must honestly disclose that my greatest source of joy comes through the knowledge that I am a child of God. Knowing that we are all beloved children of an omnipotent, constant, and loving God is the driving force behind all that I do.

Thank you for coming on this journey with me. I hope that you have found ways to increase the joy in your life. As you do, please share these experiences! I am always grateful to hear from my readers through my website: www.AliMcJoy.com. If you have found any value from my book, please consider gifting it to your friends and family. If you have received this as a gift, know that you are loved. The world is such a better place when it is filled with joy.

Joy on!

12

About the Author

Alissa McClure is a wife to her best friend {since 2003} and a grateful mother to four boys {2009, 2009, 2010, 2012) and one girl {2015}. And if you're going to be friends, you should know she has a deep and abiding love of chocolate. She's survived poverty, infertility, IVF, two NICUs, cloth diapers, food allergies, several hurricanes, and so much more! In 2017, she officially began writing and publishing children's books and LOVES it!

When she's not writing or picking her kids up from school, she'd like to be reading, singing, laughing, napping, traveling, crafting, or learning something new. But in reality, she's probably grocery shopping, cleaning something, or telling her boys to stop fighting. She lives in Katy, Texas, blogs at AliMcJoy.com, and occasionally visits Instagram {alimcjoy}, Pinterest {AliMcJoy}, and Facebook {@alimcjoy}. She is a big believer in living life–especially mothering–with intention. If she's learned anything it's that accidental success is a myth: decisions determine destiny. She will also be the first to tell you she is not even close to perfect, but she's giving life her best shot one jam-packed day at a time.

Her children's book titles are *A Nace's Adventure* and *Oggie the Otter*. At the time of this publishing, she is working on her first middle grade novel.

Visit her blog at www.AliMcJoy.com!

13

Acknowledgments

I am incredibly grateful for my beautiful, supportive family. While I wrote the pages of this book in the early morning hours of school days, I formatted it and organized the bulk of it at our kitchen table, surrounded by the chaos that naturally ensues when you have five young children running around in the same household. I am grateful for the opportunity I have been given to be their mother. I am grateful for an incredibly supportive husband who works side-by-side with me as we try to succeed in parenting, while he simultaneously gives me the encouragement and support I need to pursue my own dreams. He is more than I could have ever imagined. I am blessed to have an amazing group of people who subscribe to my weekly newsletters and who follow me on social media. I am so grateful for their kind words and support. Without them, I don't know if I would have the courage to keep trying. With them, I feel like I can keep my heart pounding through my fingers, onto the keyboard, producing words and sentences and paragraphs.

Thank you for taking the time to read my words. I hope that they have brought more joy to your life. I honestly believe that is the biggest reason we exist: to have joy.

Joy on, dear friend.

Thanks for reading!

And thank you for helping me with my goal to bring more joy into the world.

www.ingramcontent.com/pod-product-compliance
Lightning Source LLC
Chambersburg PA
CBHW060529030426
42337CB00021B/4191